99 dead snowmen

First published in 2012
by HEADLINE PUBLISHING GROUP

1

Cataloguing in Publication Data is available from the British Library

Hardback ISBN 978 0 7553 6384 1

Printed in Italy by L.E.G.O. S.p.A.

Headline's policy is to use papers that are natural, renewable and recyclable products and made from wood
grown in sustainable forests. The logging and manufacturing processes are expected to conform to the
environmental regulations of the country of origin.

HEADLINE PUBLISHING GROUP
An Hachette UK Company
338 Euston Road
London NW1 3BH

www.headline.co.uk
www.hachette.co.uk

99 dead snowmen

TONY DE SAULLES

headline

for joe

www.tonydesaulles.co.uk
http://twitter.com/TonyDeSaulles

Enormous thanks to my literary agent, Sarah Such, for helping bring 99 Dead Snowmen to life and also to Sarah and Richard at Headline for their enthusiasm and belief in the book. Thanks also to my walking mate, Ben, who 'got it' immediately and suggested endless scenarios as we trekked up various mountains. And a final big thank you to my wife, Janet, whose patience and support enables me to follow my arty ambitions.

1. death by cup of tea

2. death by evil robins

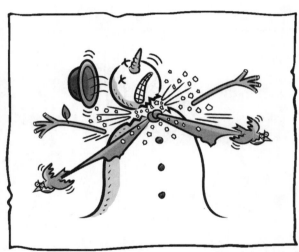

3. death by mole

4. death by dog

5. death by Level crossing

6. death by microwave

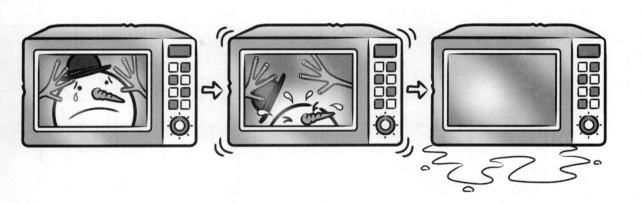

7. death by skydiving

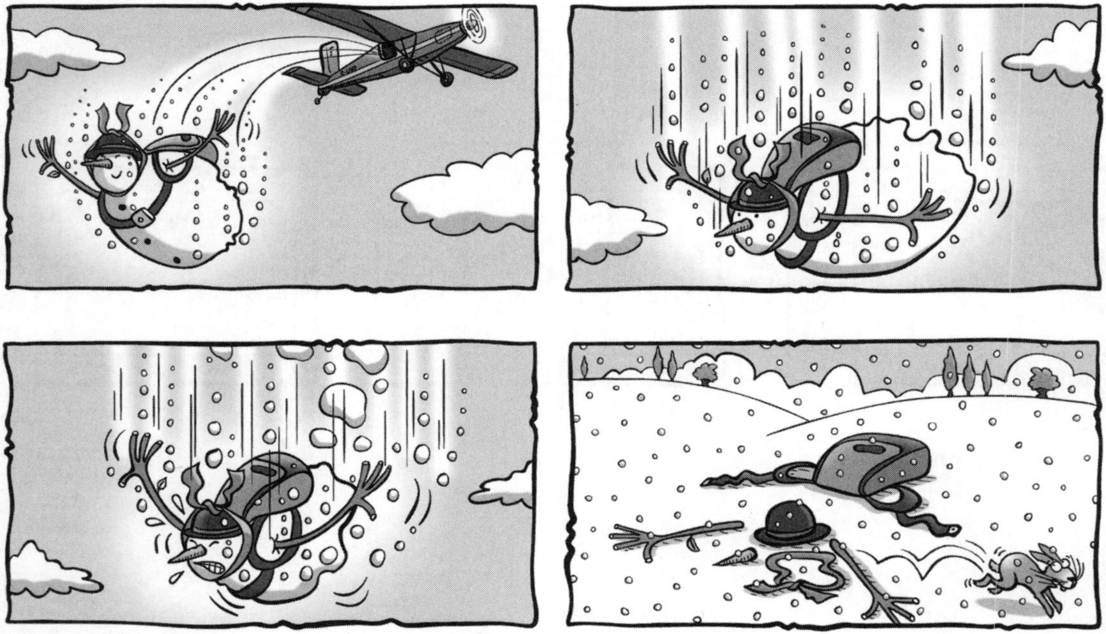

8. death by william tell

9. death by football

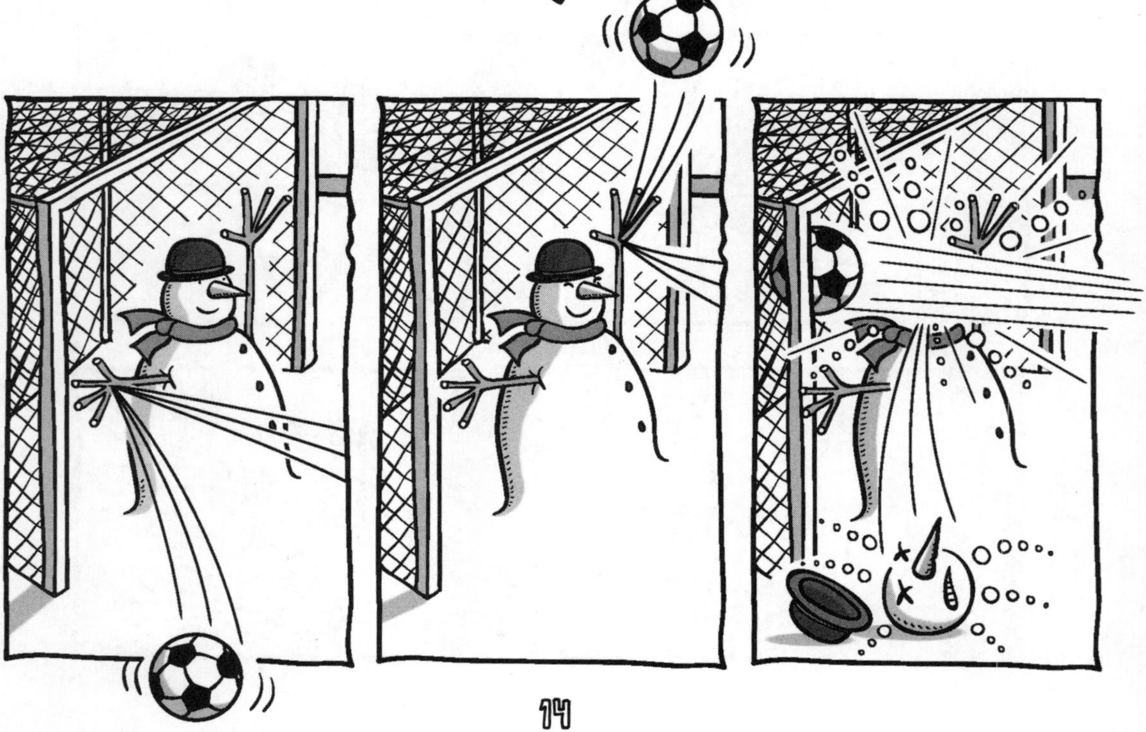

10. death by dad

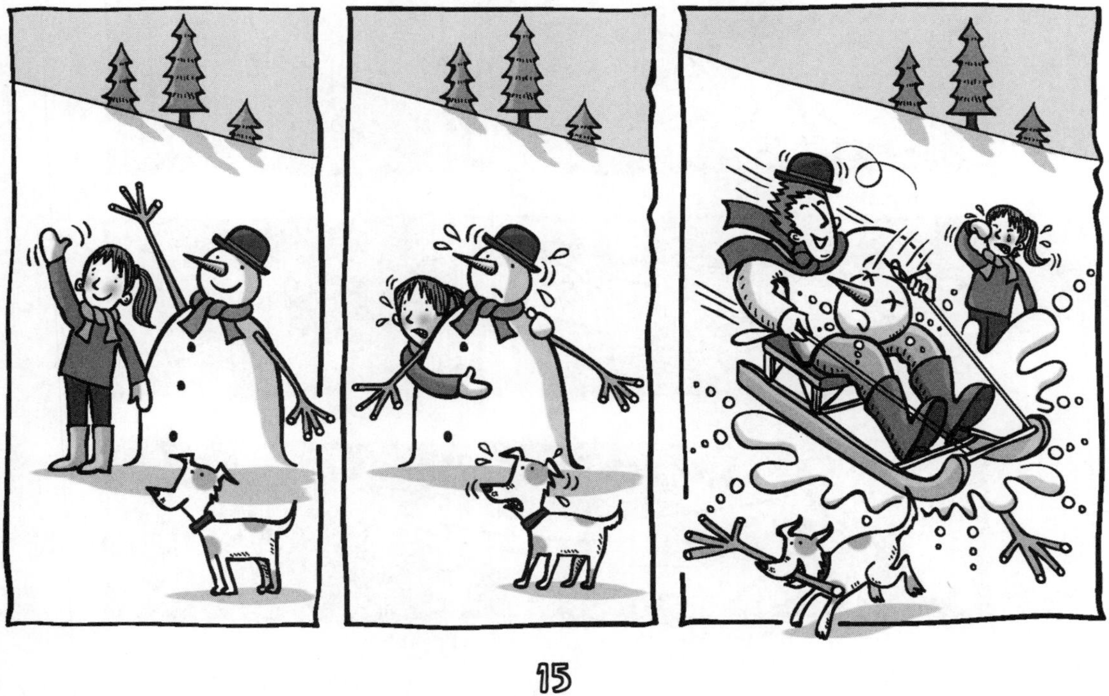

11. death by aliens (no.1)

12. death by chocolate flake

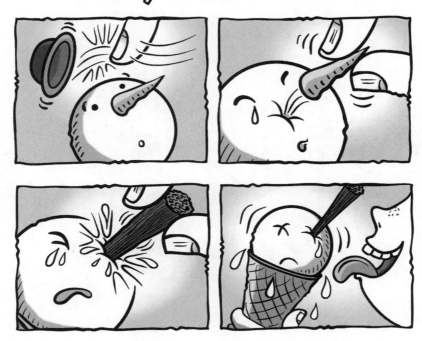

13. death by cannibals

14. death by sneezing

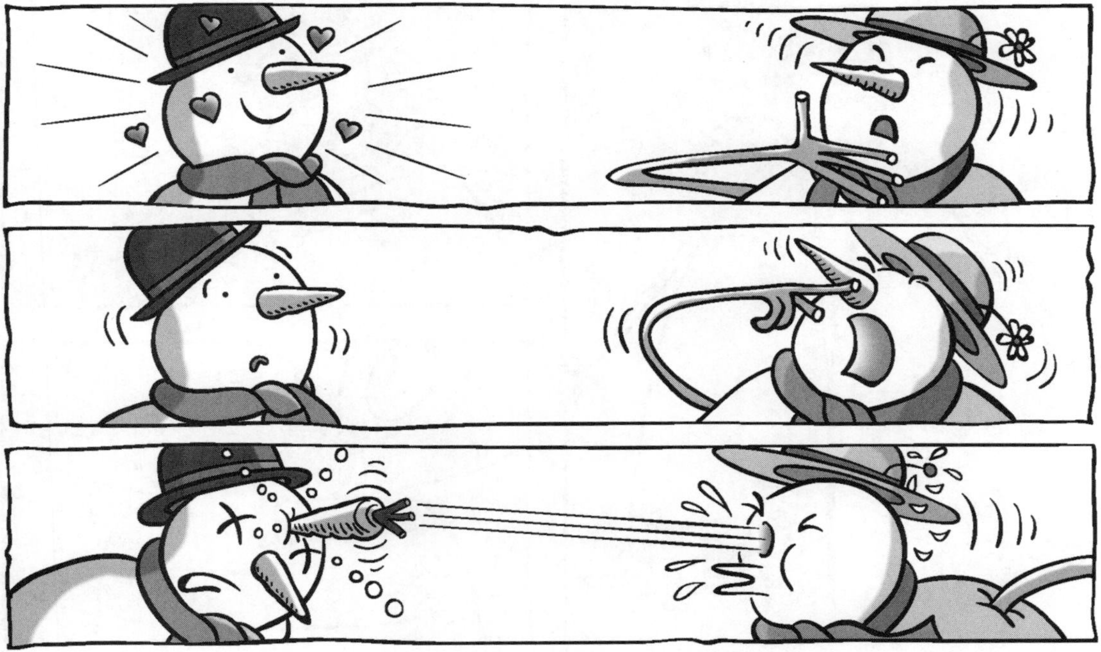

15. death by eskimo

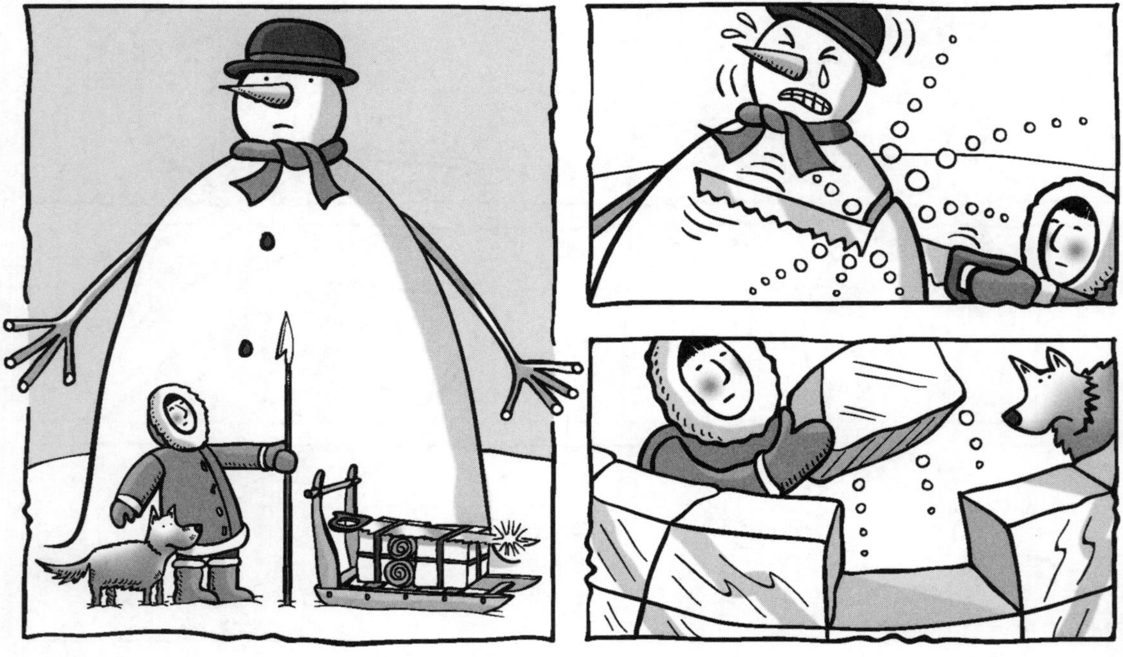

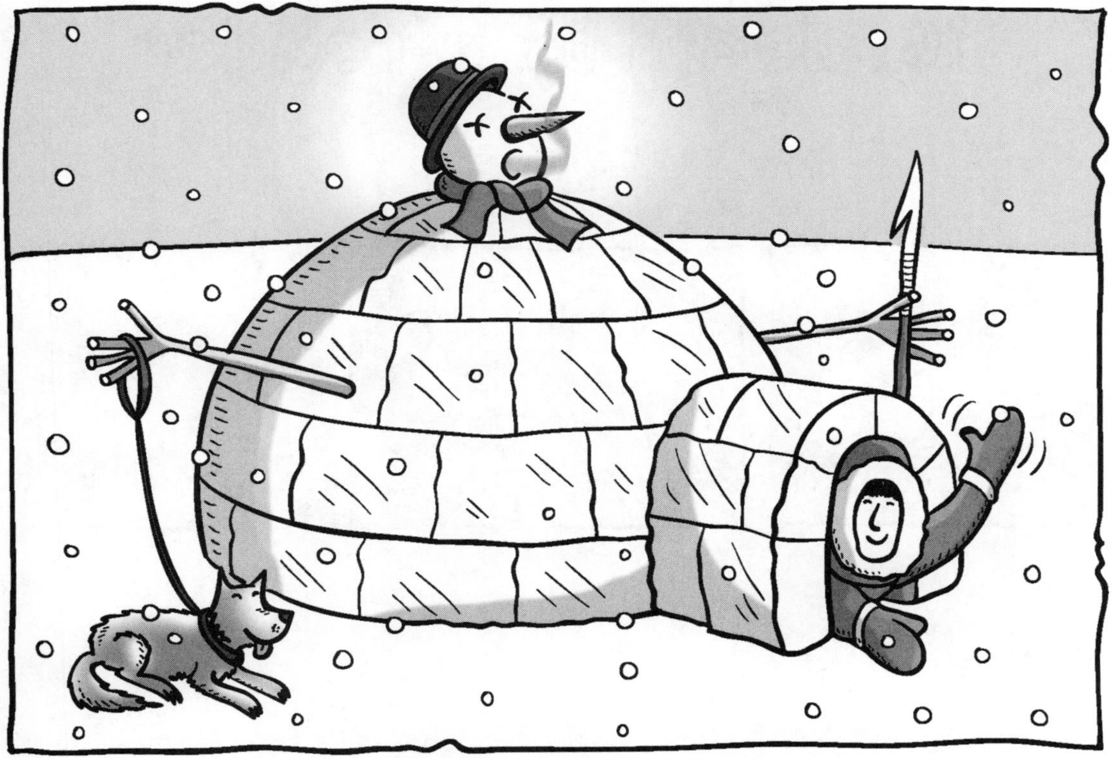

16. death by e-reader

17. death by tramp

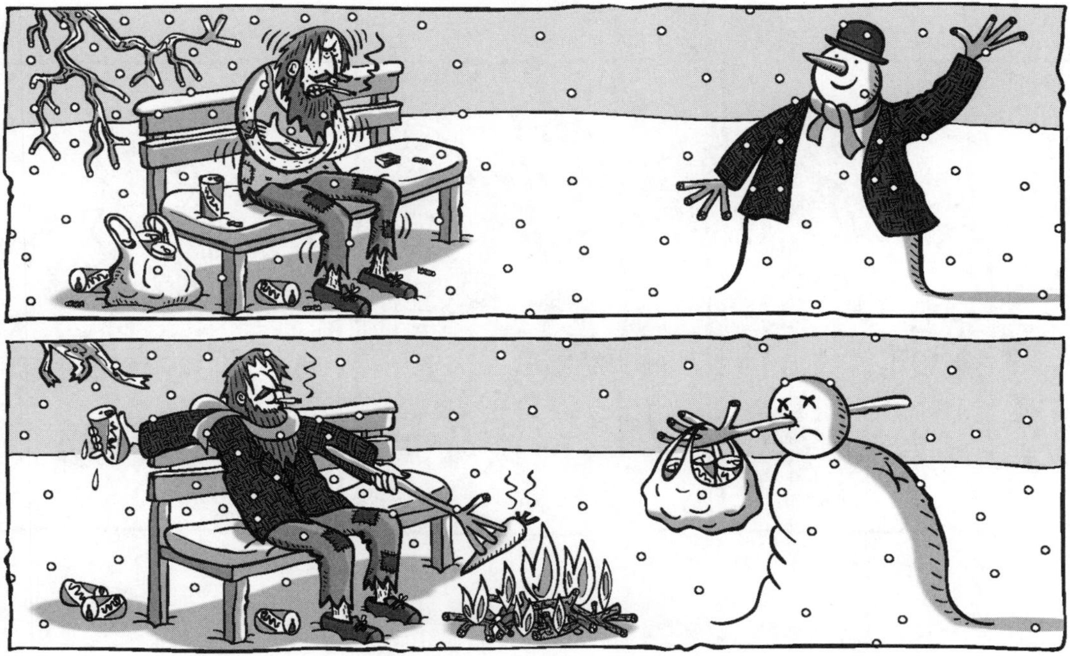

18. death by accidental prod

no.1
miss santa
modelling
competition
no.2
miss santa
modelling
competition

19. death by cat (no.1)

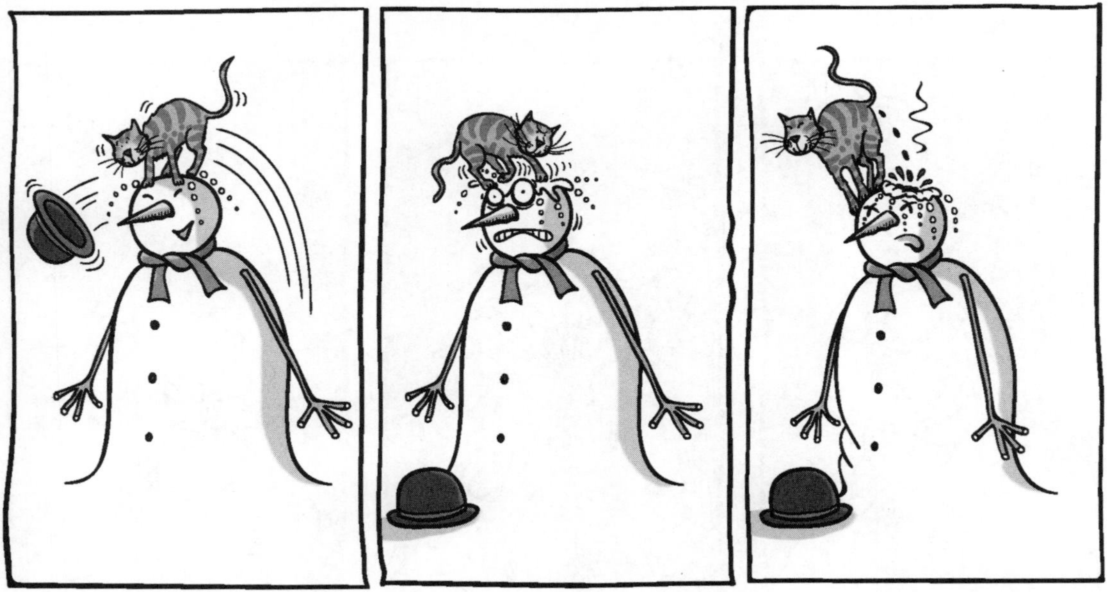

20. death by rabbit (no.1)

21. death by friendly hot-water bottles

22. death by Lonely old Lady

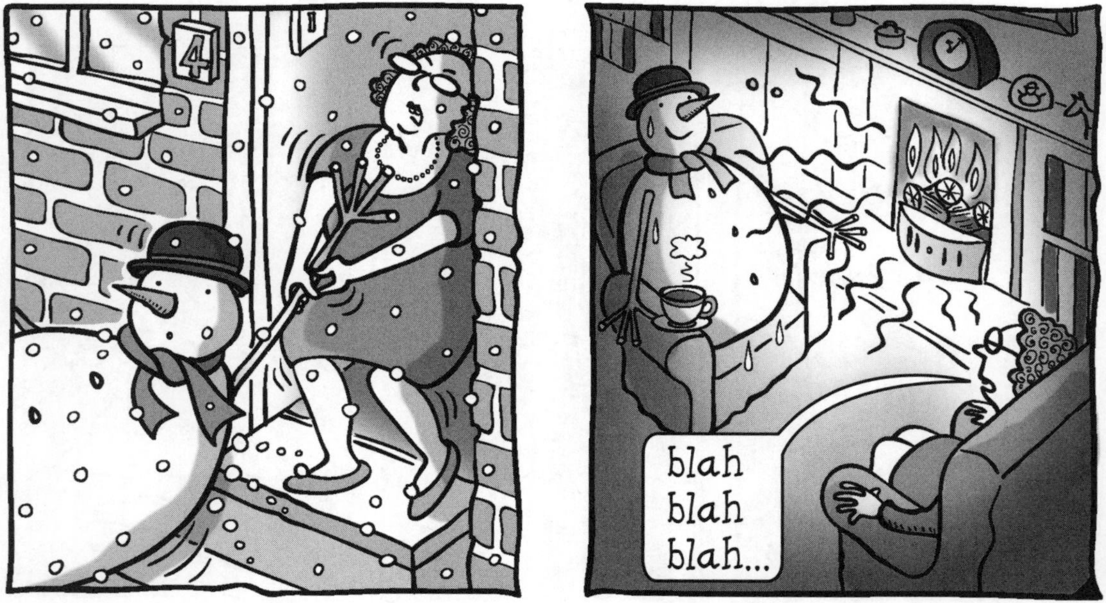
4
blah
blah
blah...

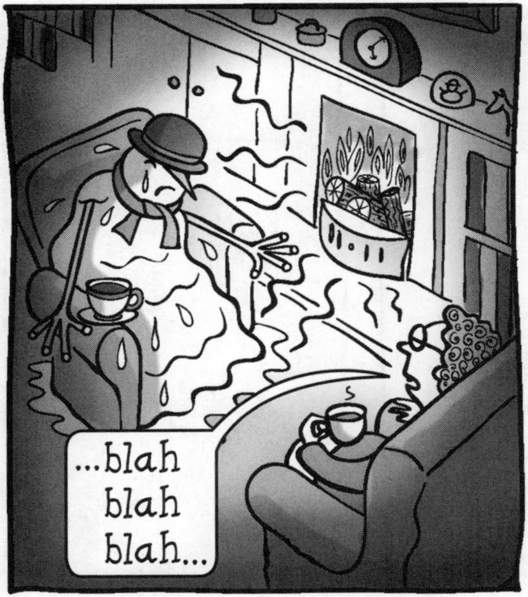
...blah
blah
blah...

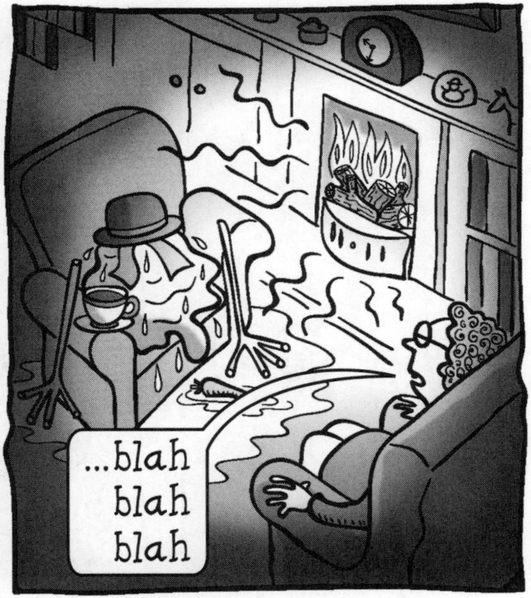
...blah
blah
blah

23. death by little girl

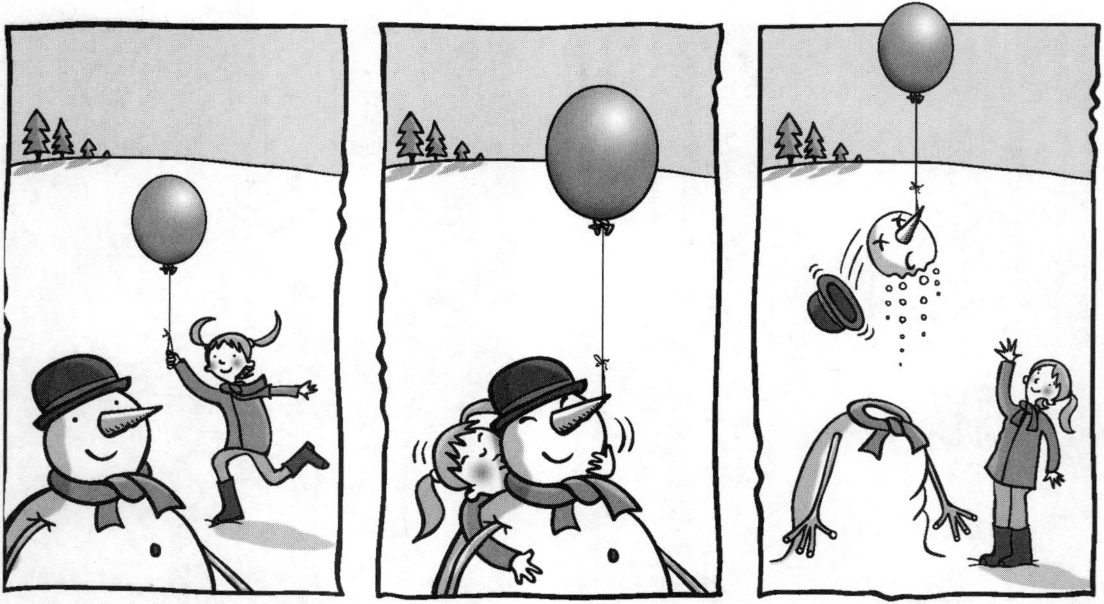

24. death by hair dryer

25. death by embarrassment

 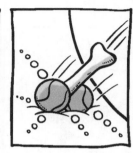

26. death by reindeer

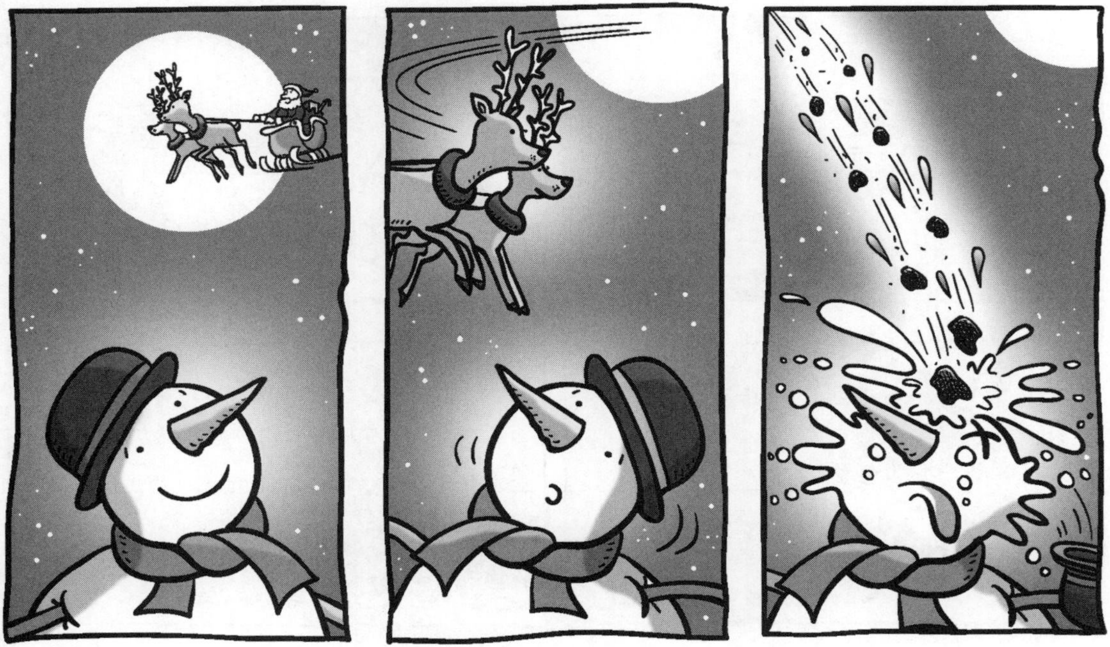

27. death by penguin

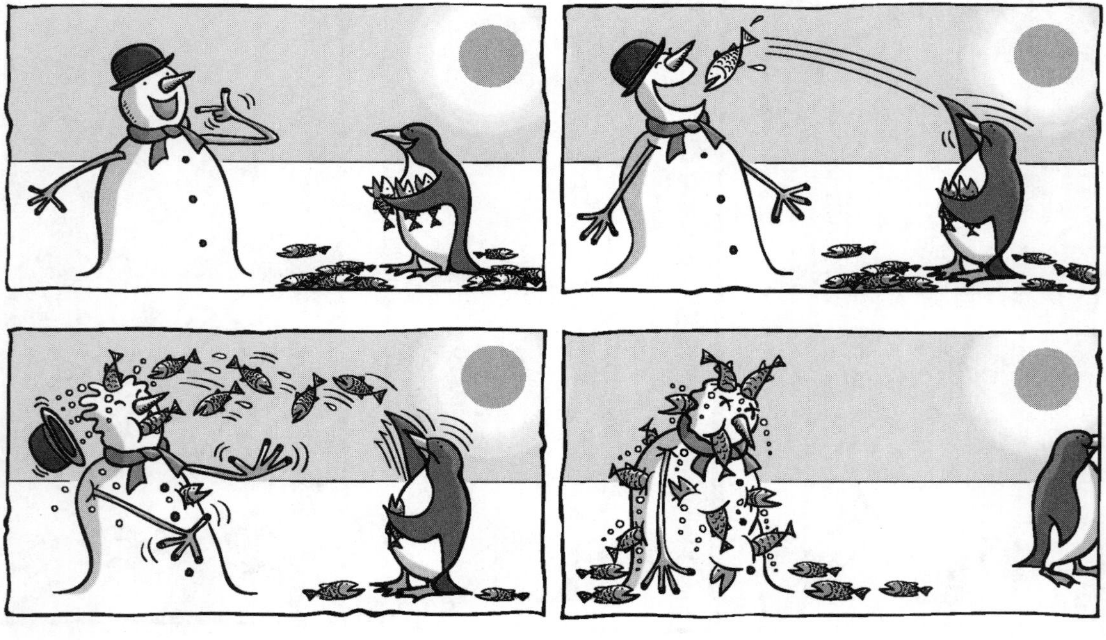

28. death by jungle

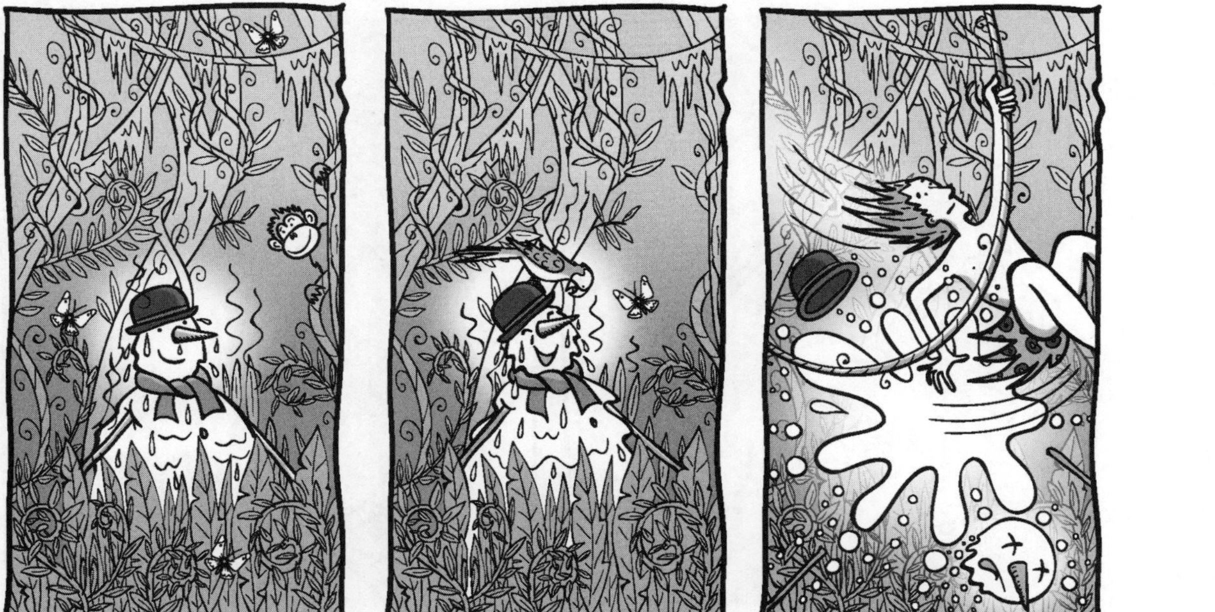

29. death by mountaineer

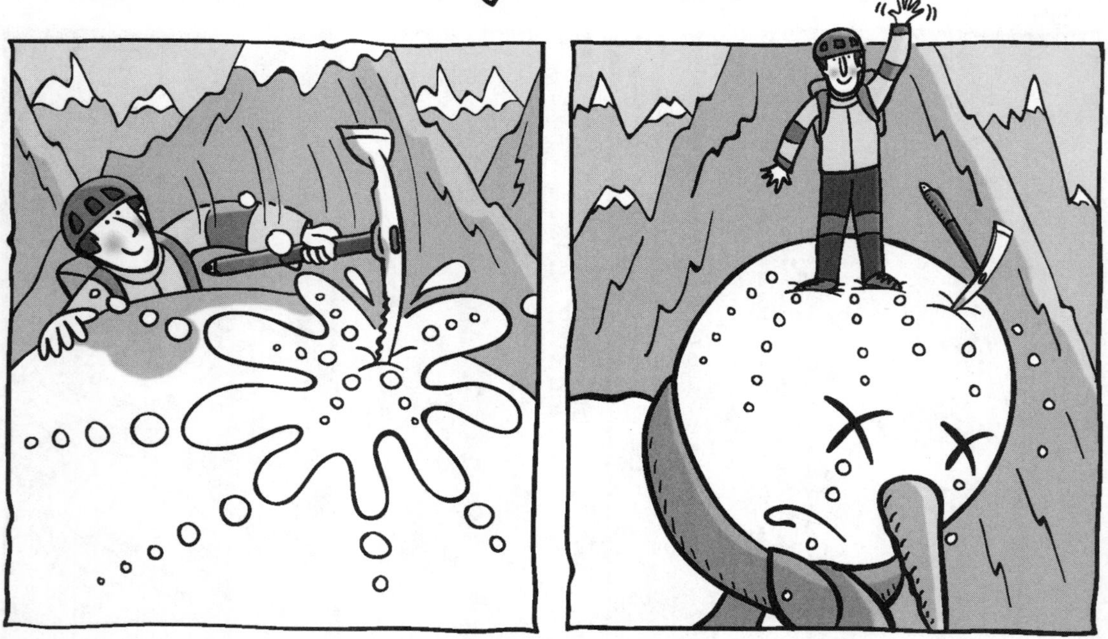

30. death by frisbee

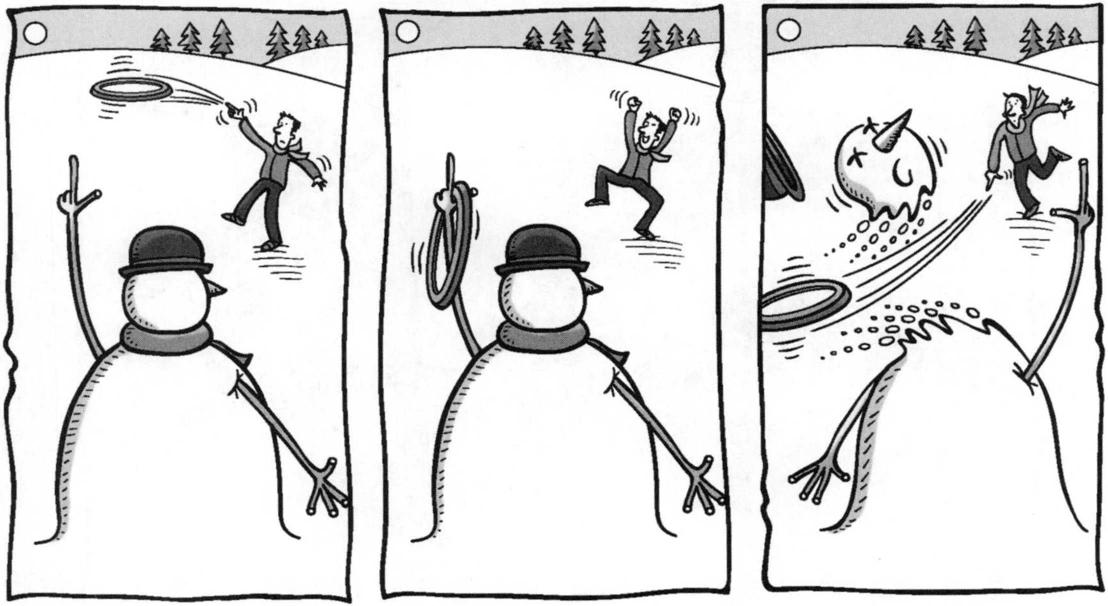

31. death by captain scott

32. death by pub

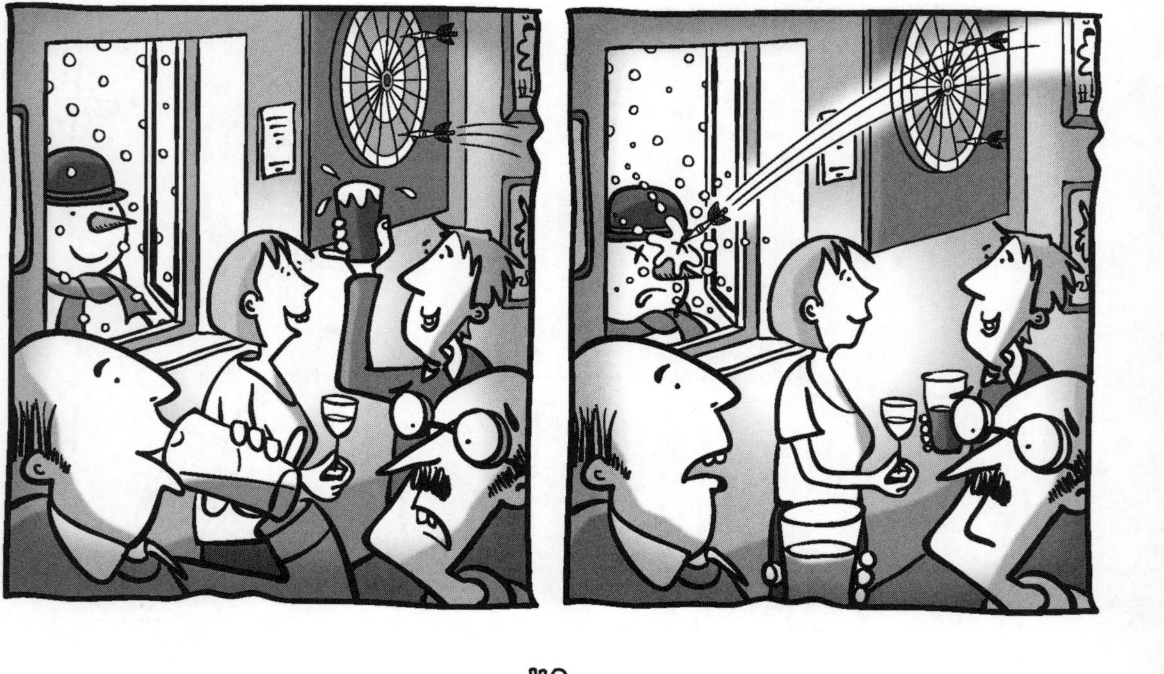

33. death by water pistol

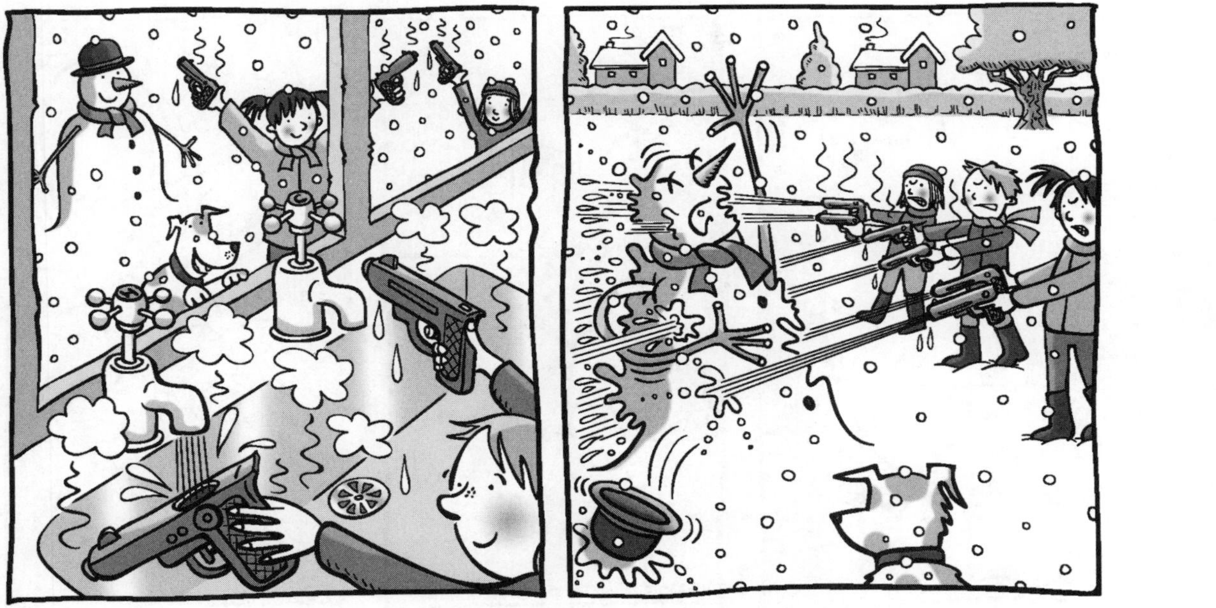

34. death by rugby

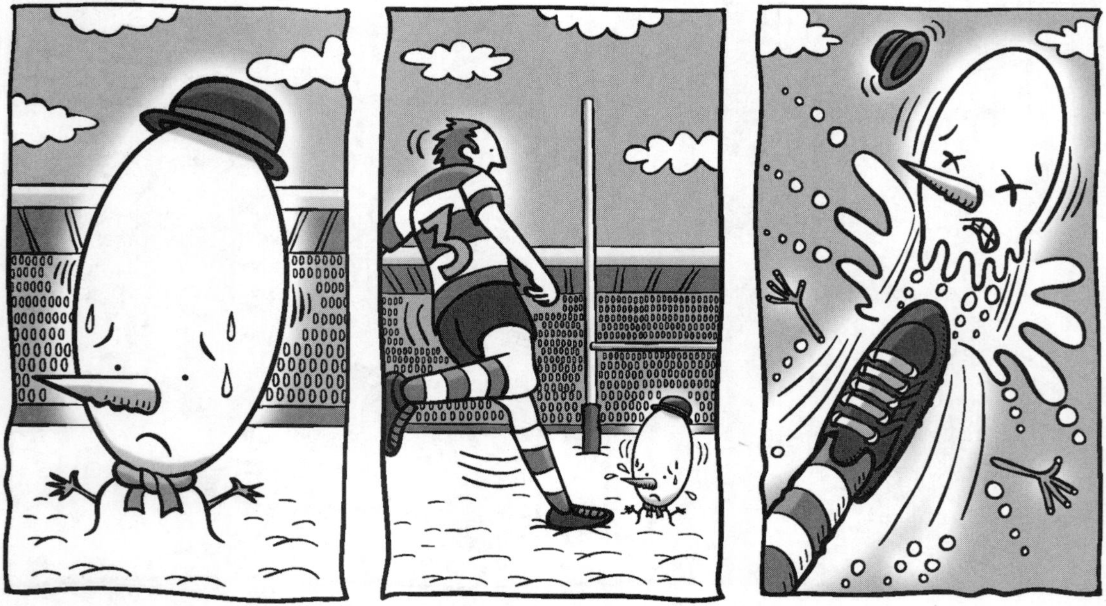

35. death by rabbit (no.2)

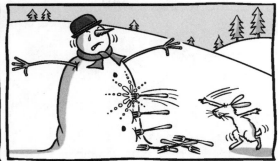

36. death by fox

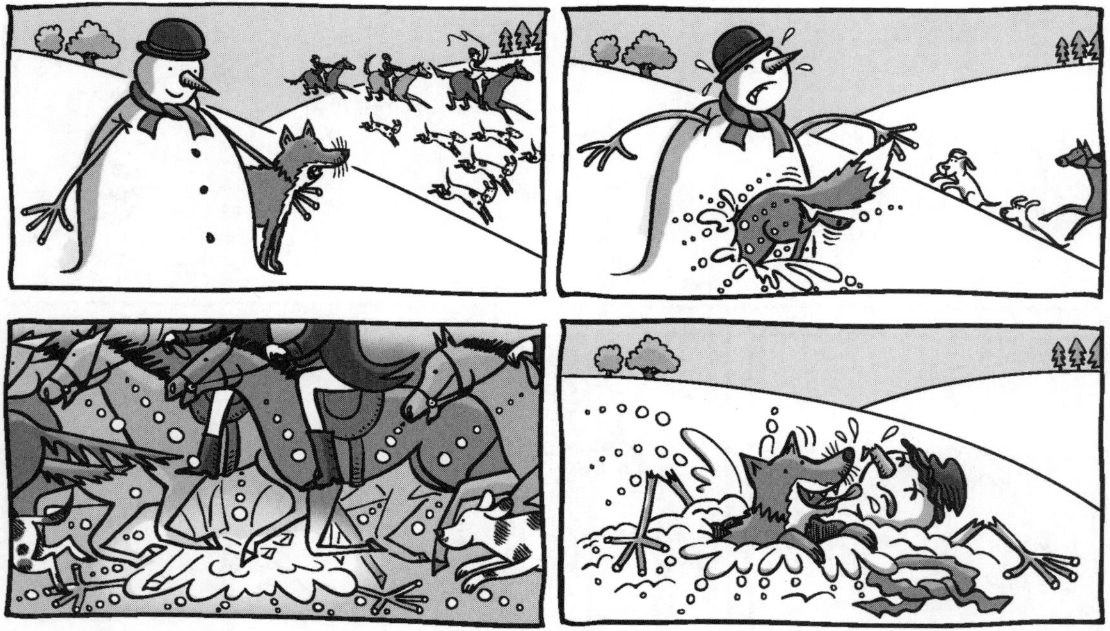

37. death by umbrella

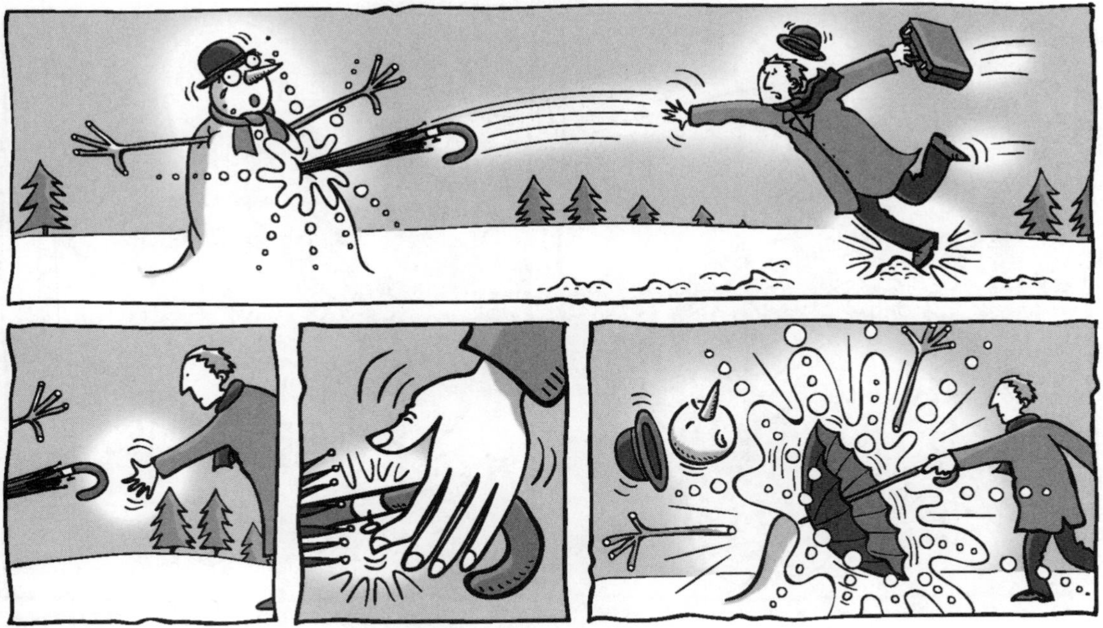

38. death by knitting

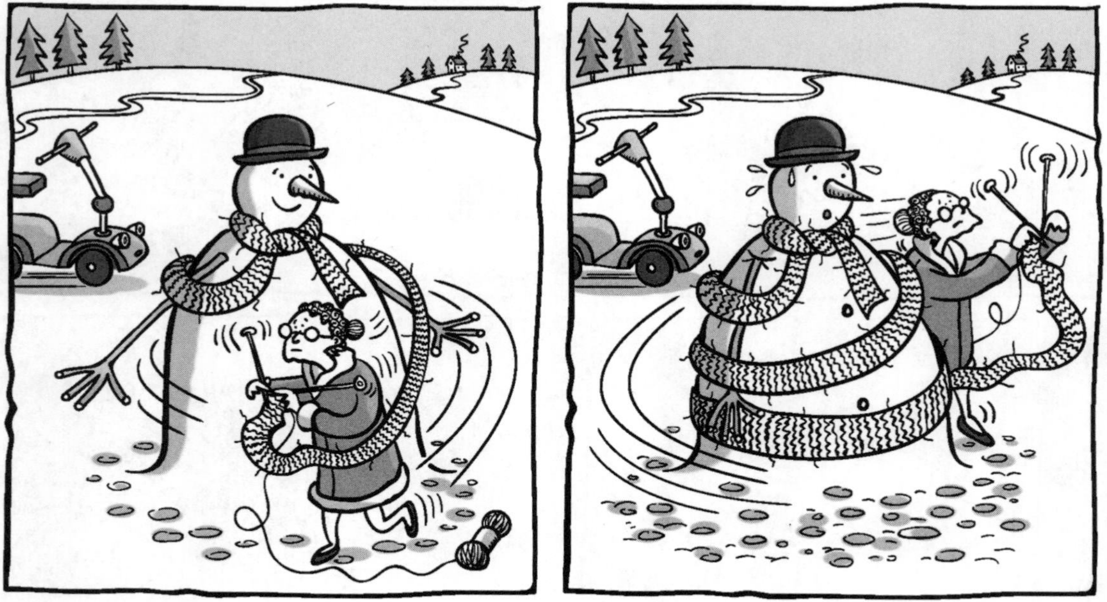

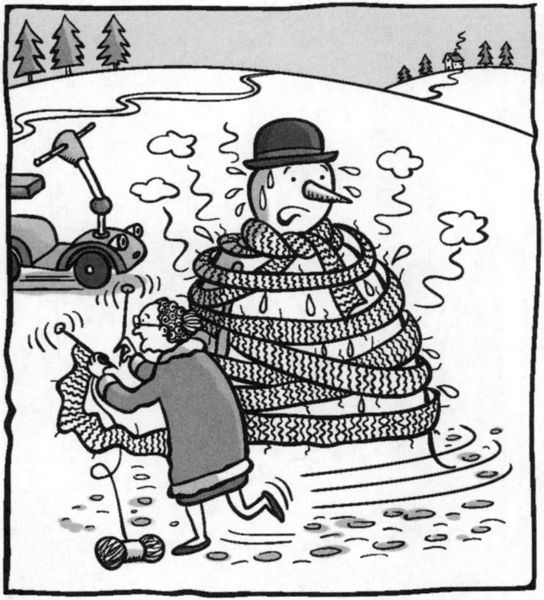

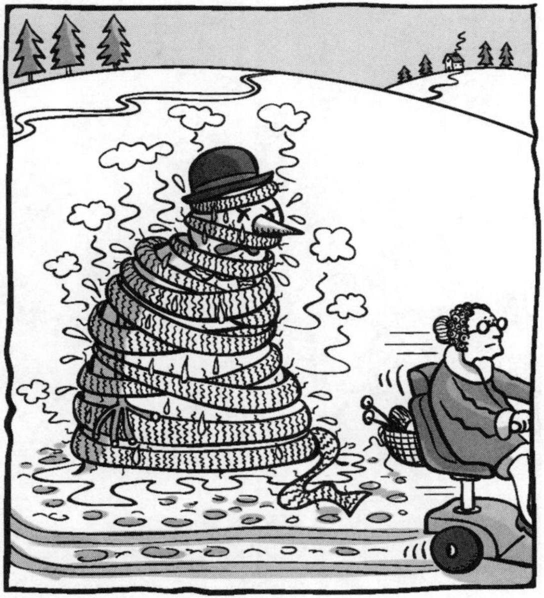

39. death by fireworks

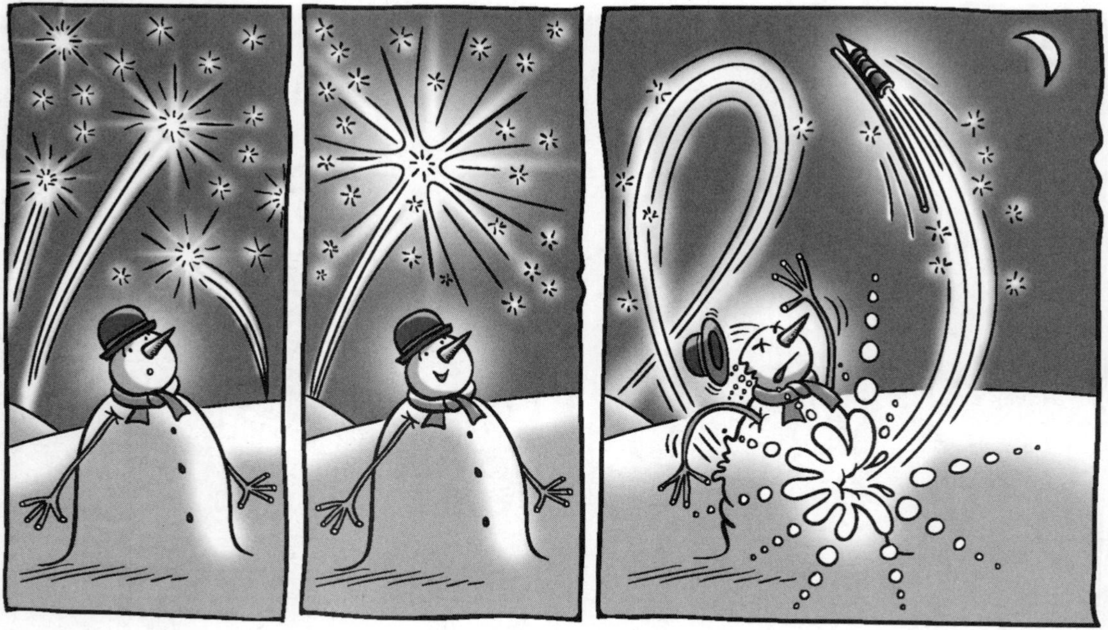

40. death by crow

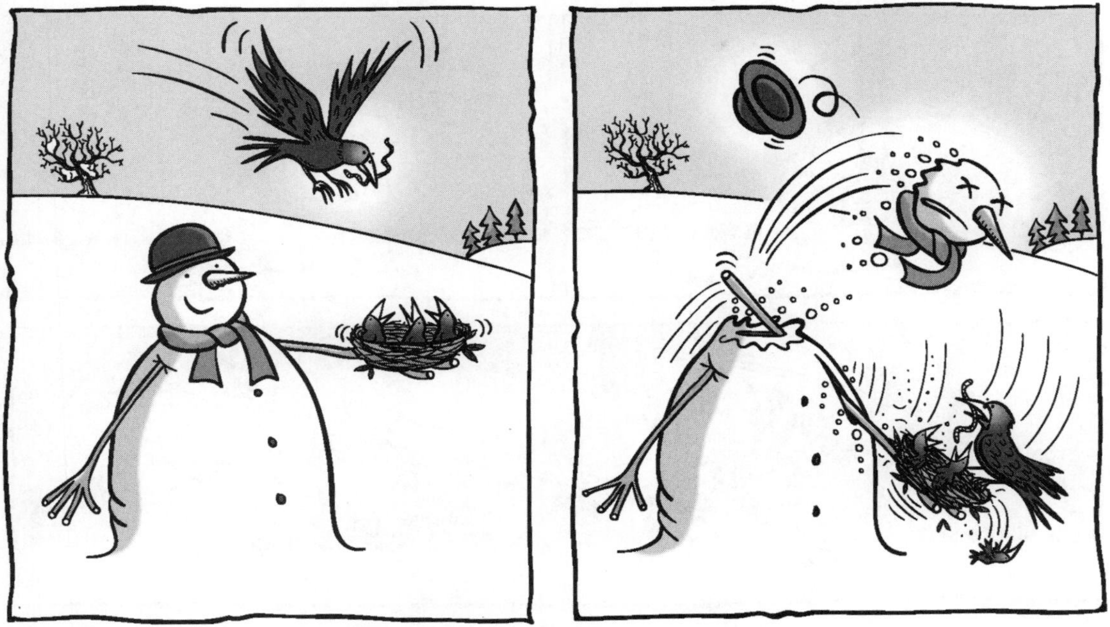

41. death by summer oLympics

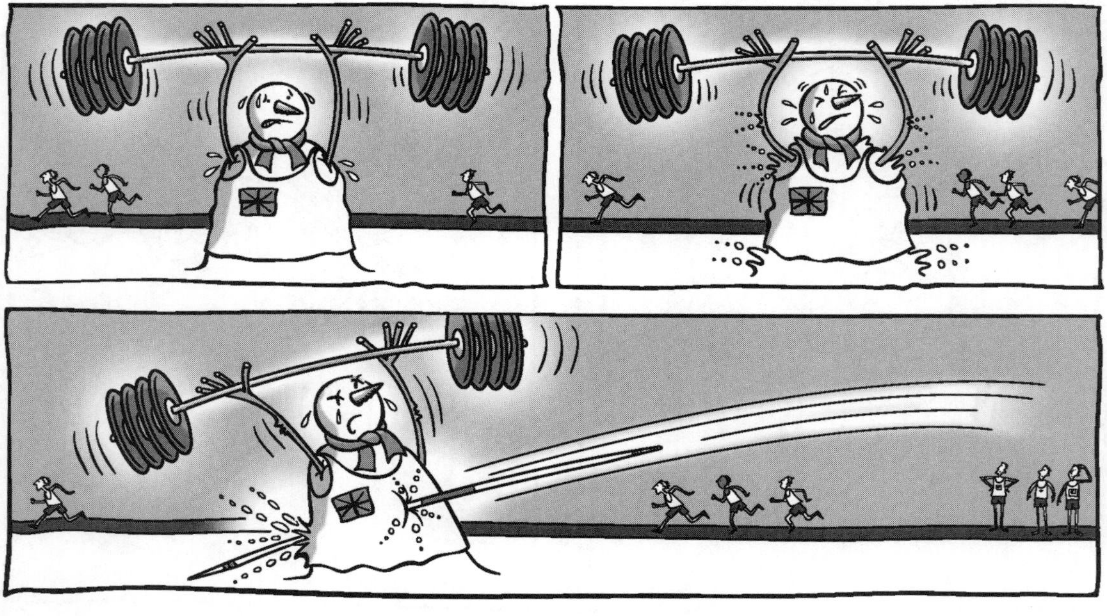

42. death by spring

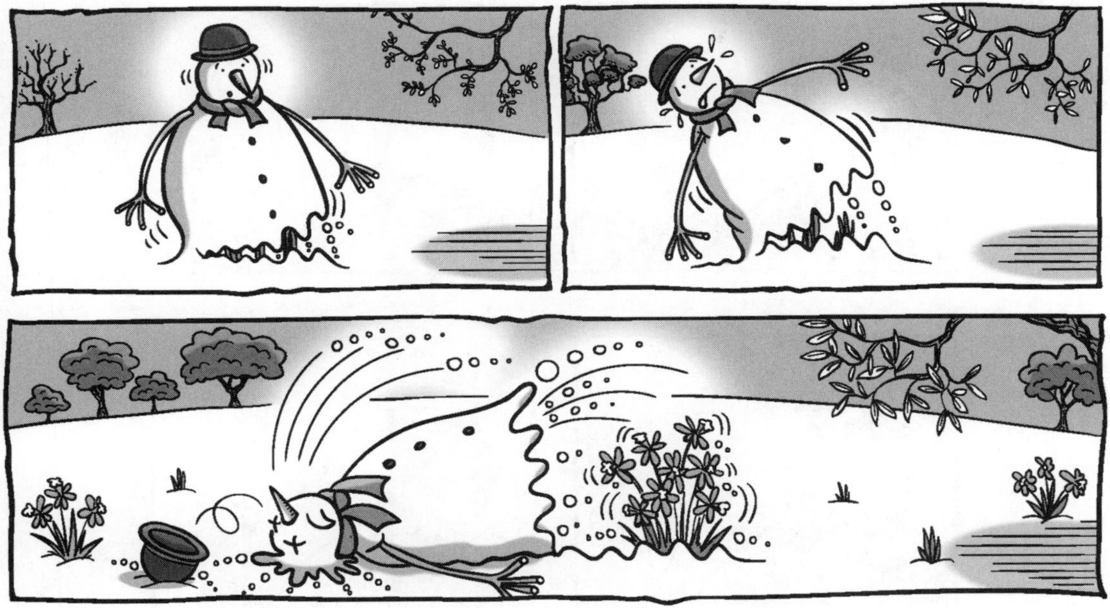

43. death by small boy

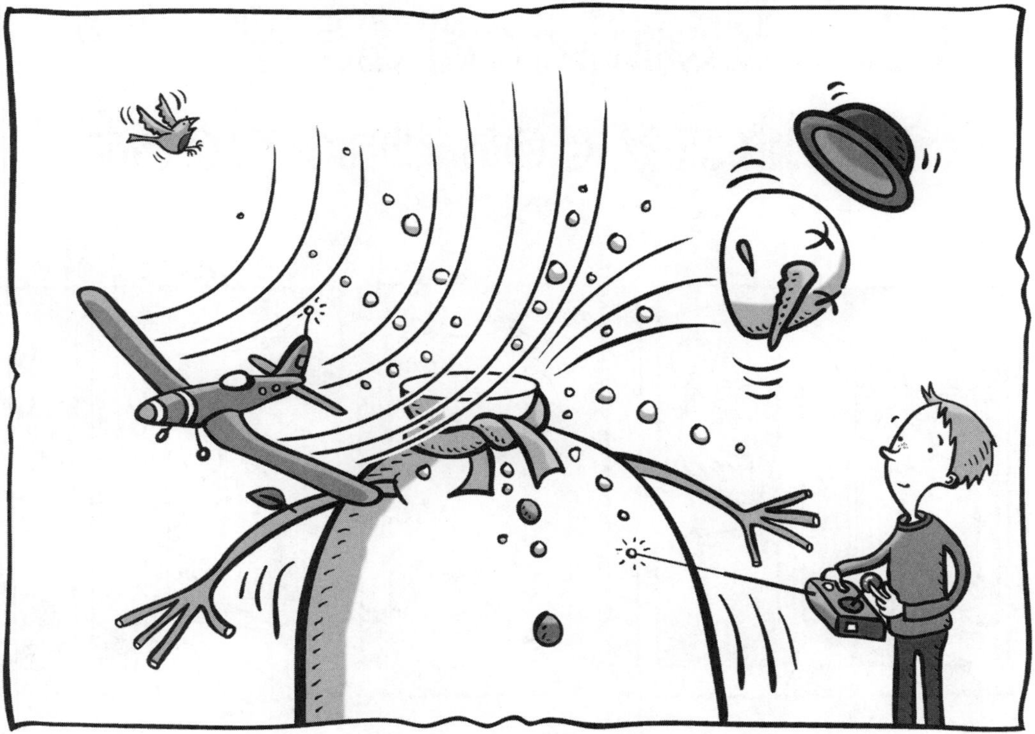

44. attempted death by solitary confinement

12 months Later...

OCT
NOV
DEC
SEP
AUG
JUL
JUN
APR
MAY
JAN
MAR
FEB

45. attempted death by iron maiden fridge

46. attempted death by warm fridge (successful)

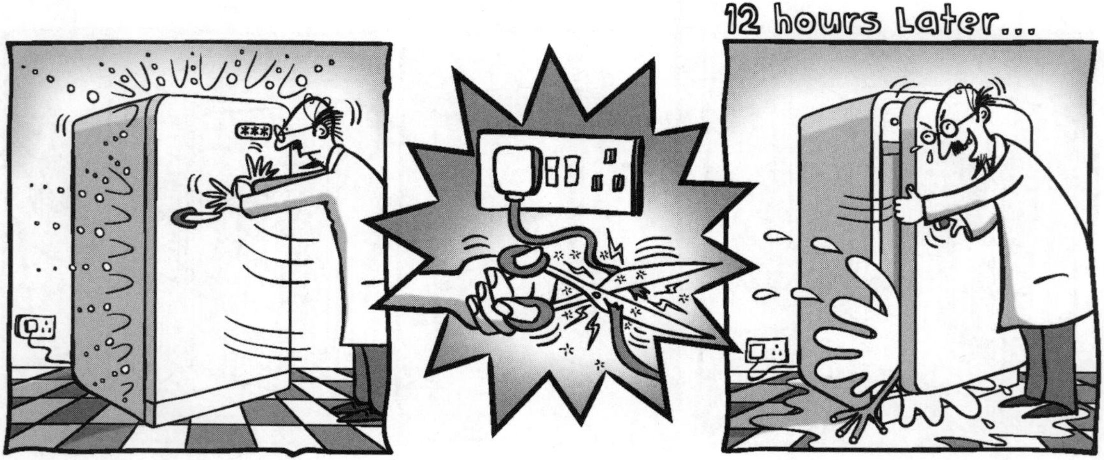
***
12 hours Later...

47. death by winter oLympics

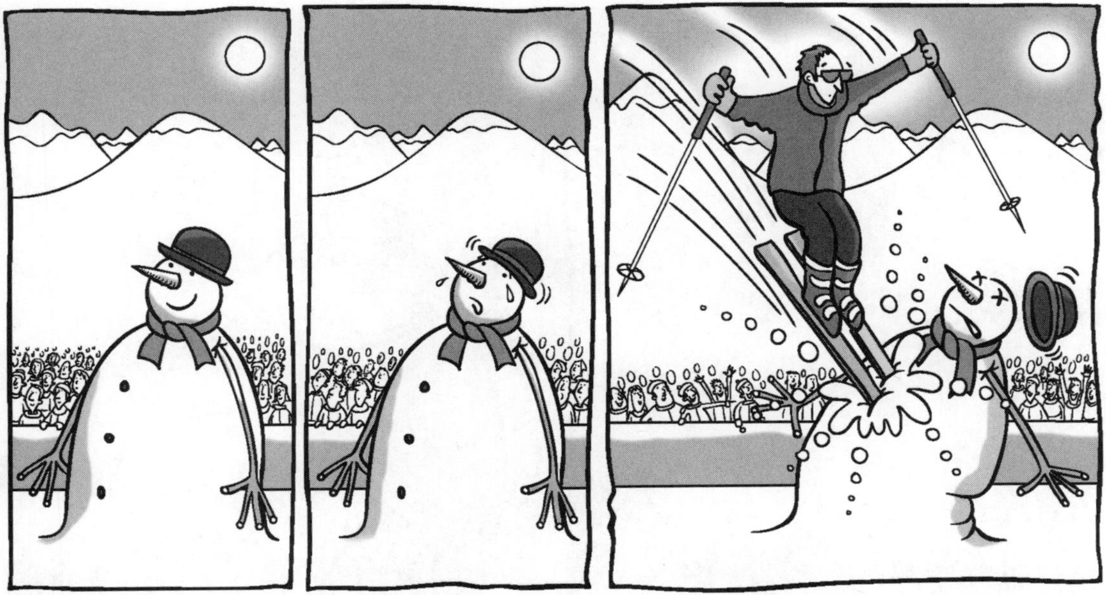

48. death by mountain rescue

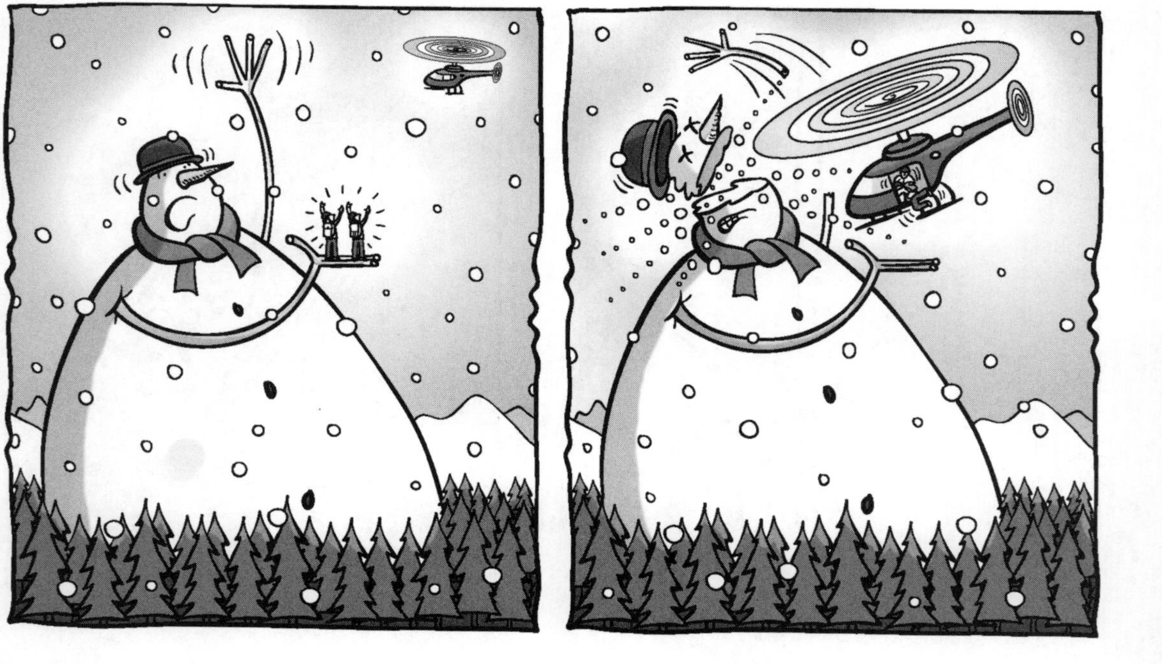

49. death by wind

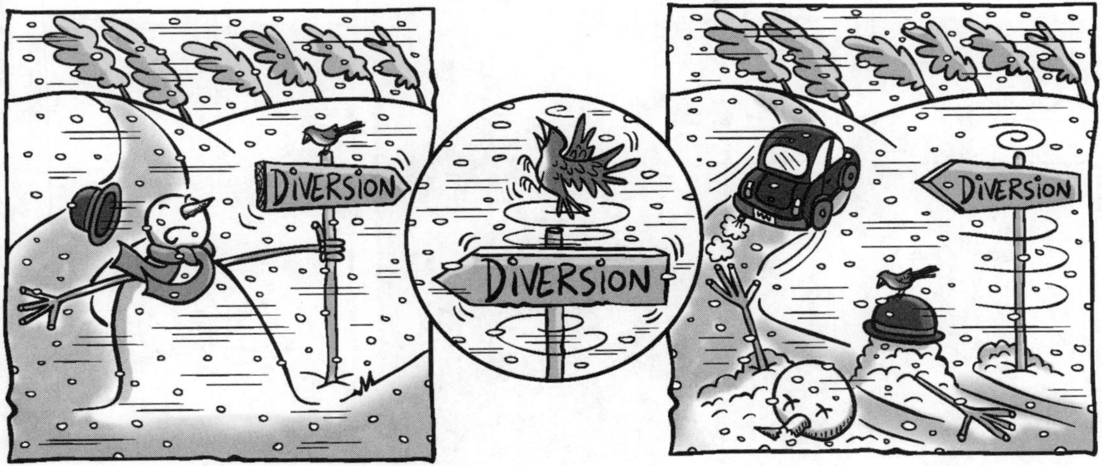
DIVERSION
DIVERSION
DIVERSION

50. death by home time

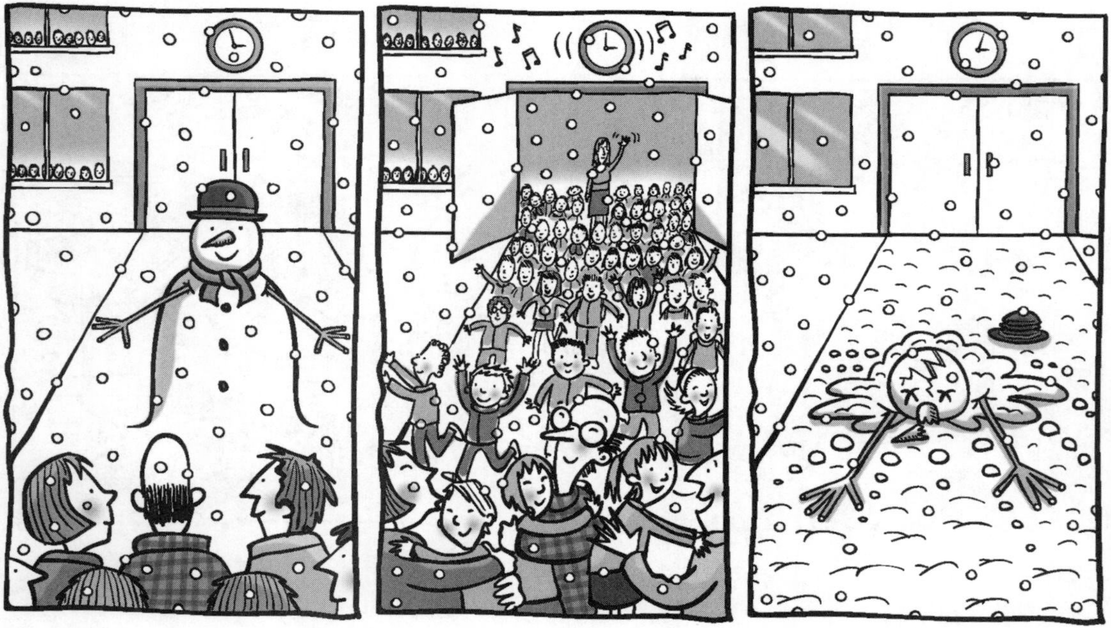

51. death by mistLetoe

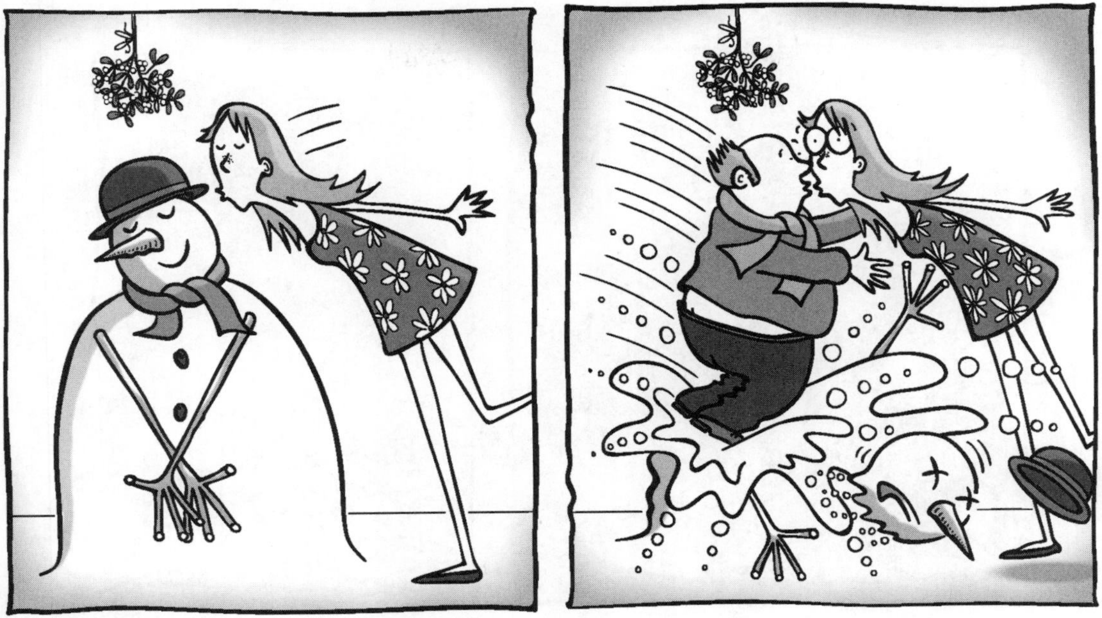

52. death by recycling

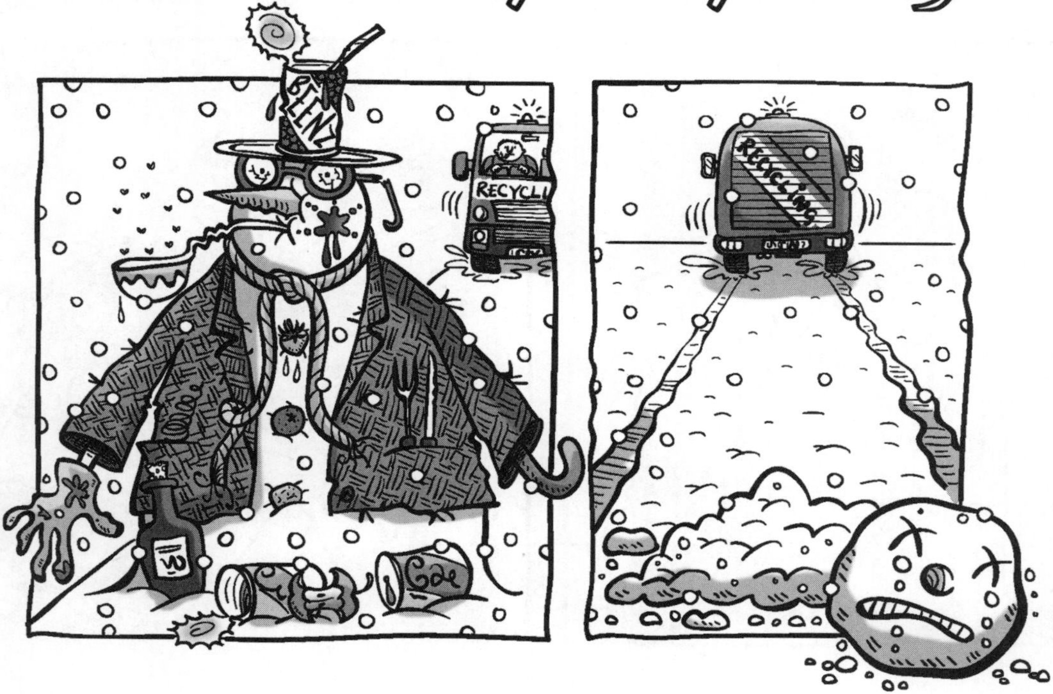
BEENZ
RECYCLI
RECYCLING
VO
Coke

53. death by january sales

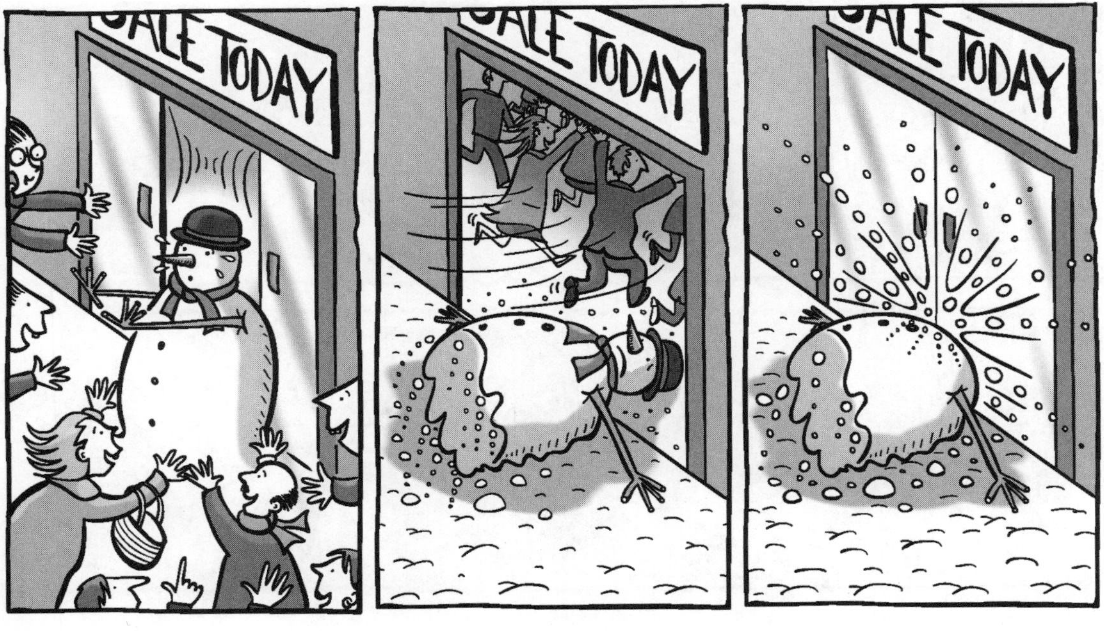
SALE TODAY
SALE TODAY
SALE TODAY

54. death by christmas tree

55. death by meteorite

 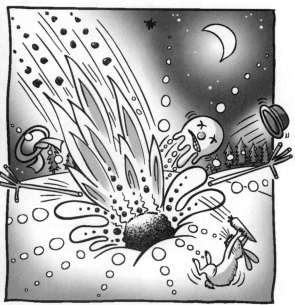

56. death by global warming

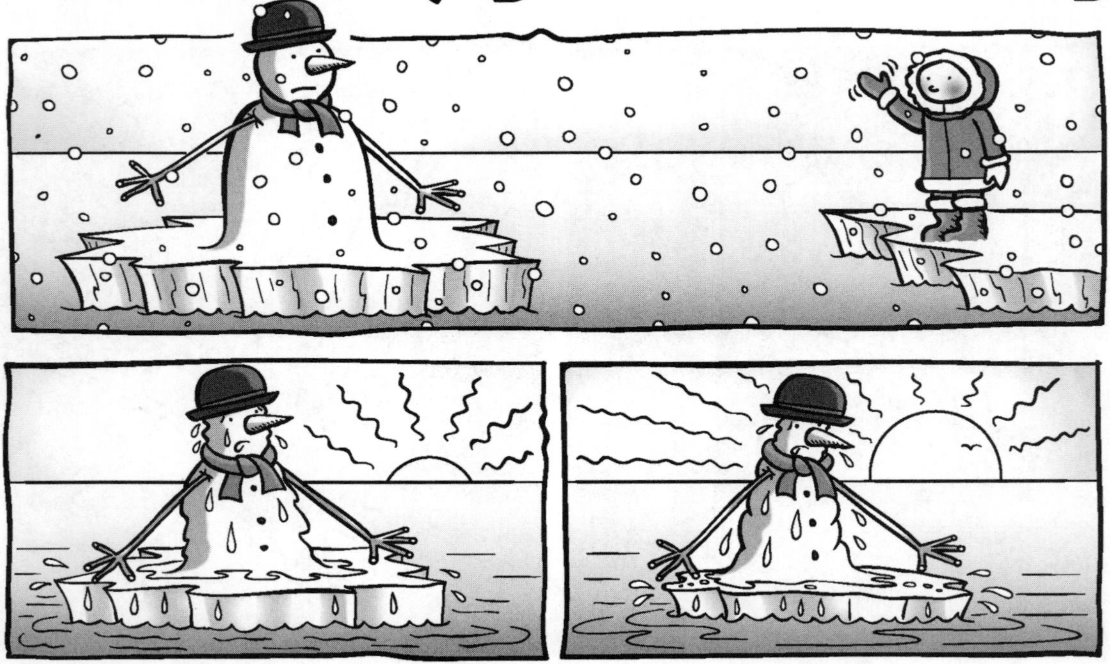

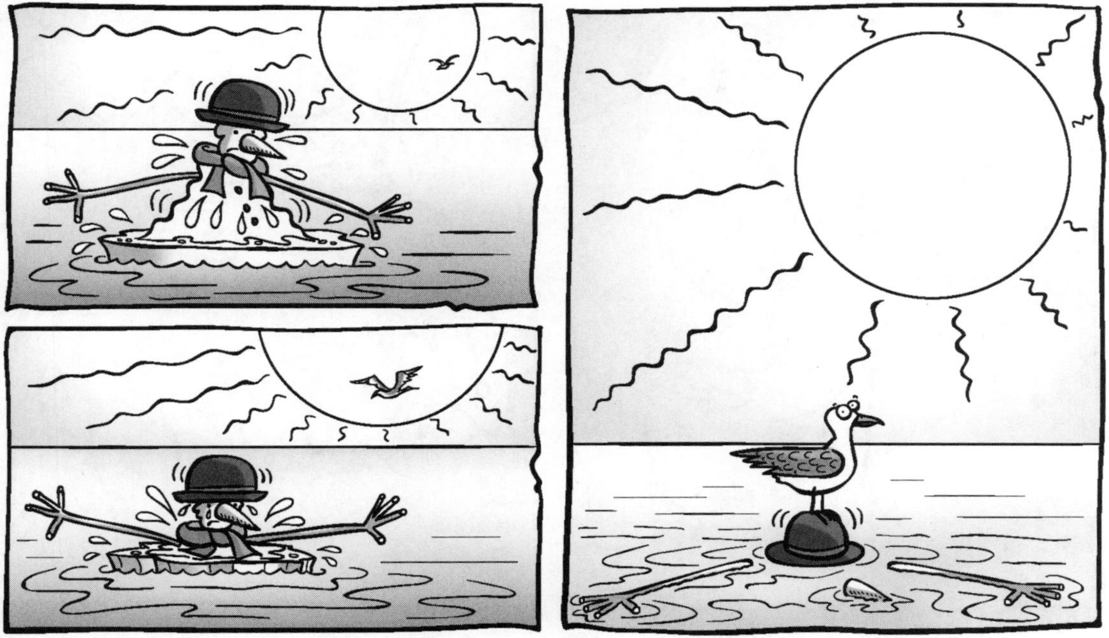

57. death by polar bear

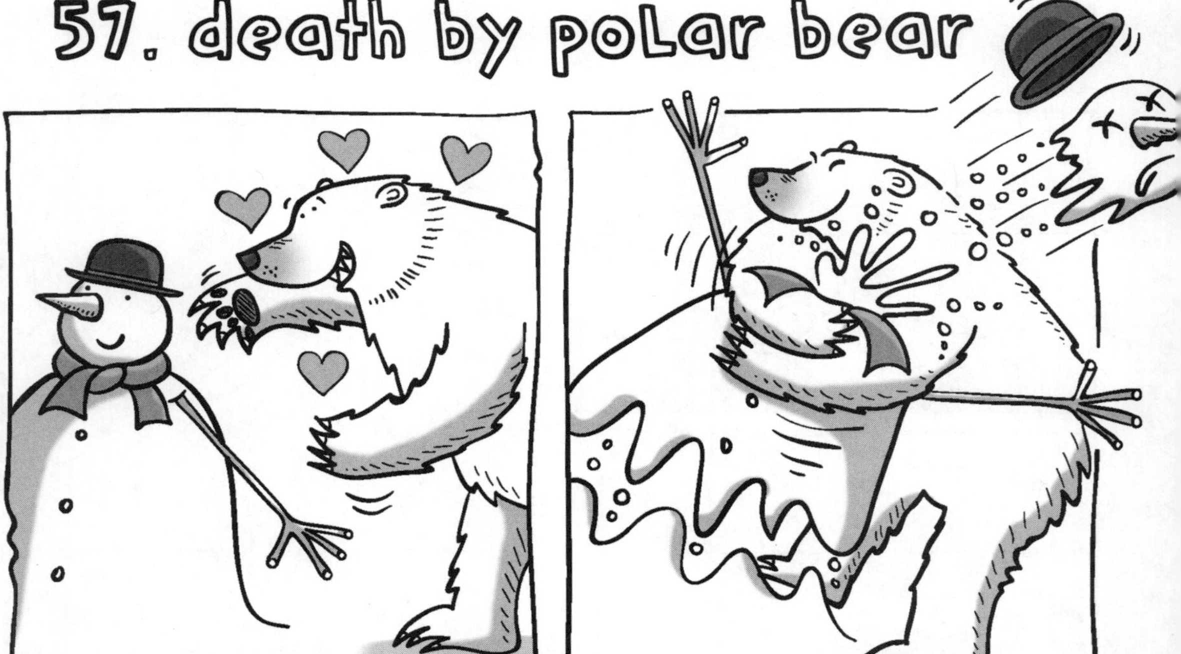

58. death by christmas cake

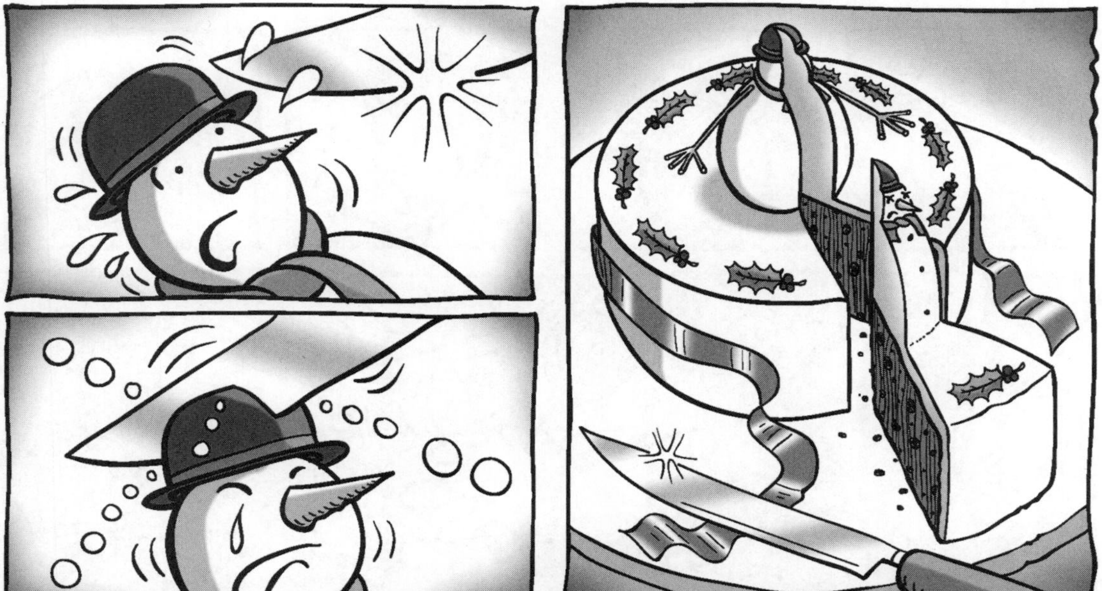

59. death by newspaper

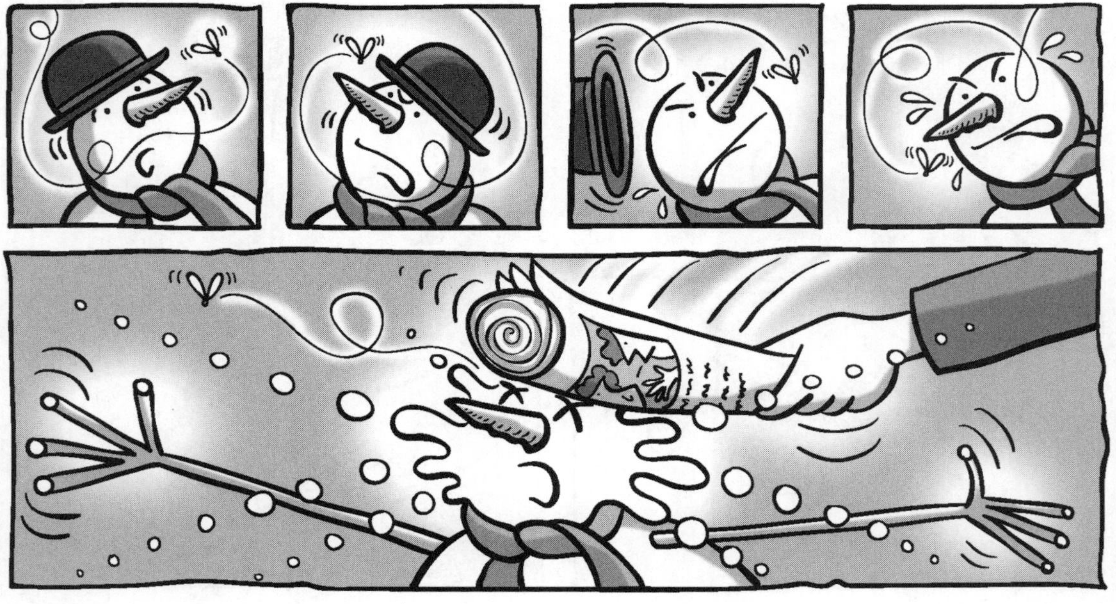

60. death by snowplough

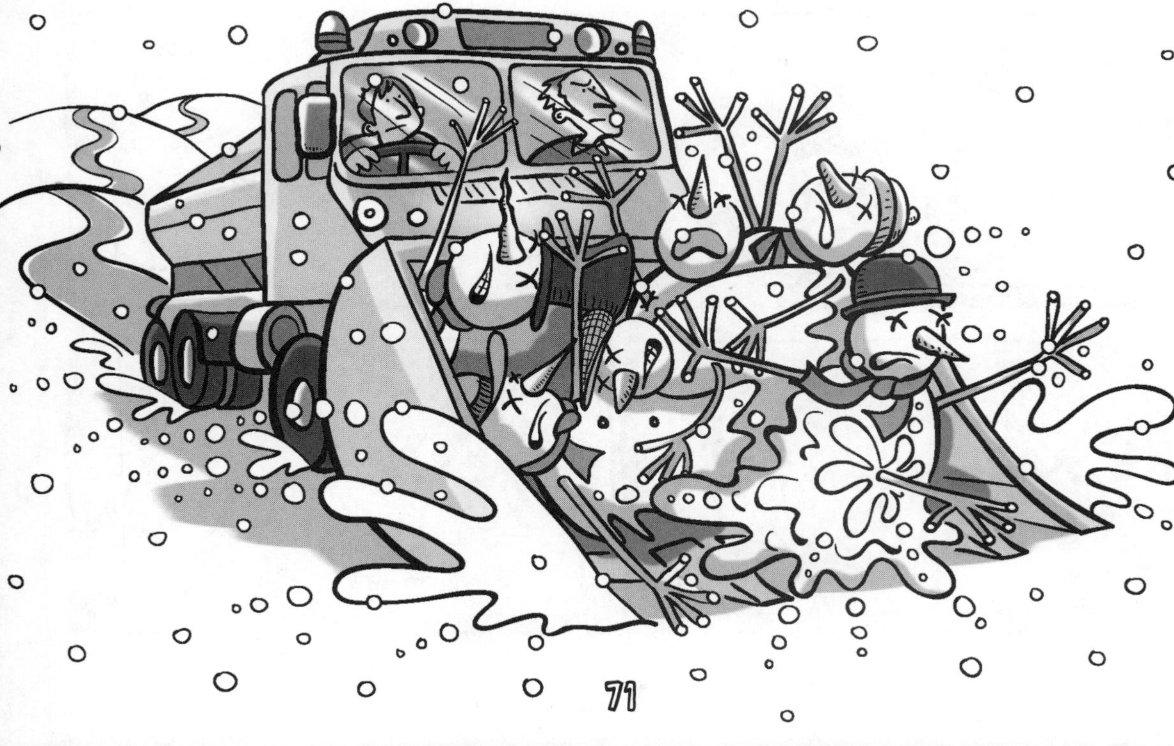

61. death by sorbet

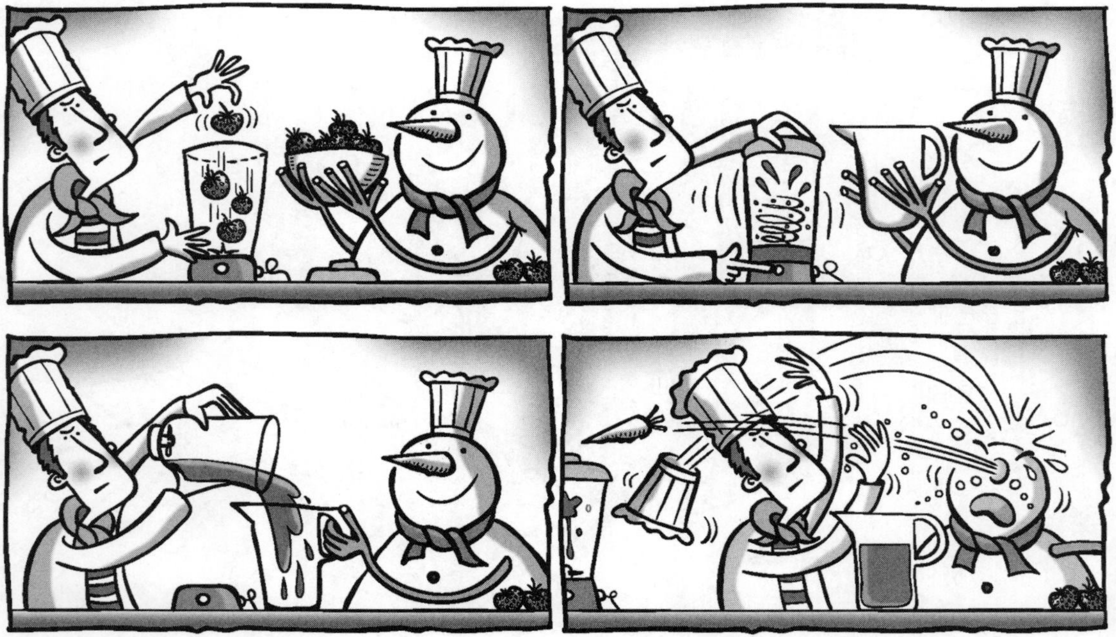

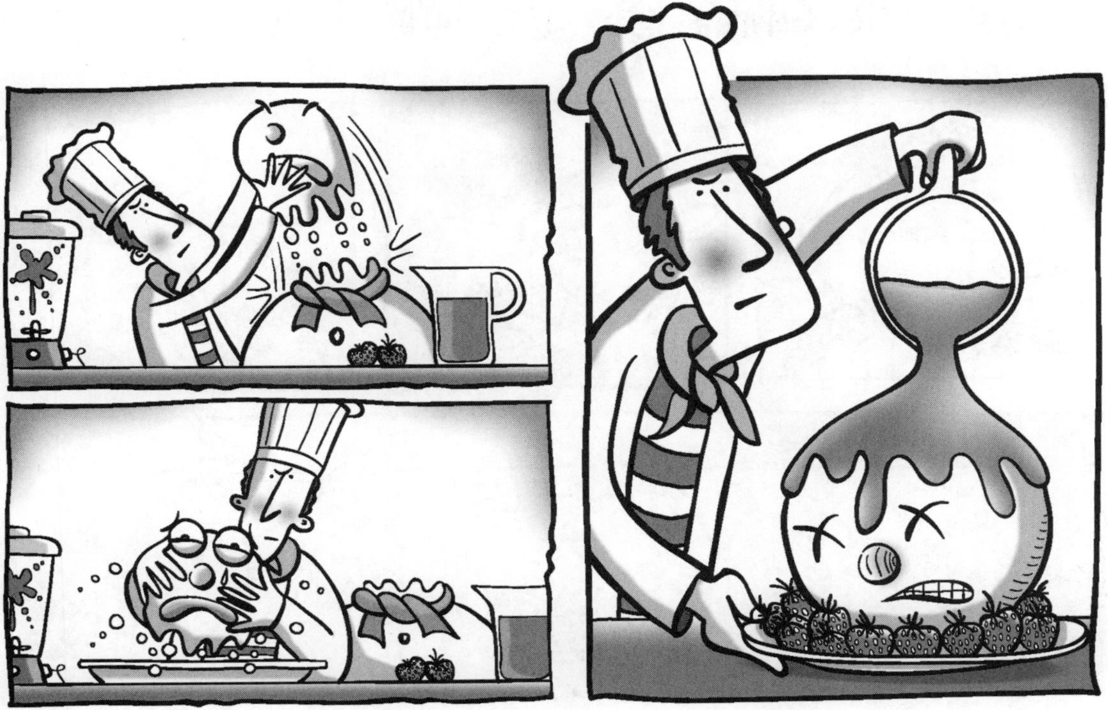

62. death by rabbit (no.3)

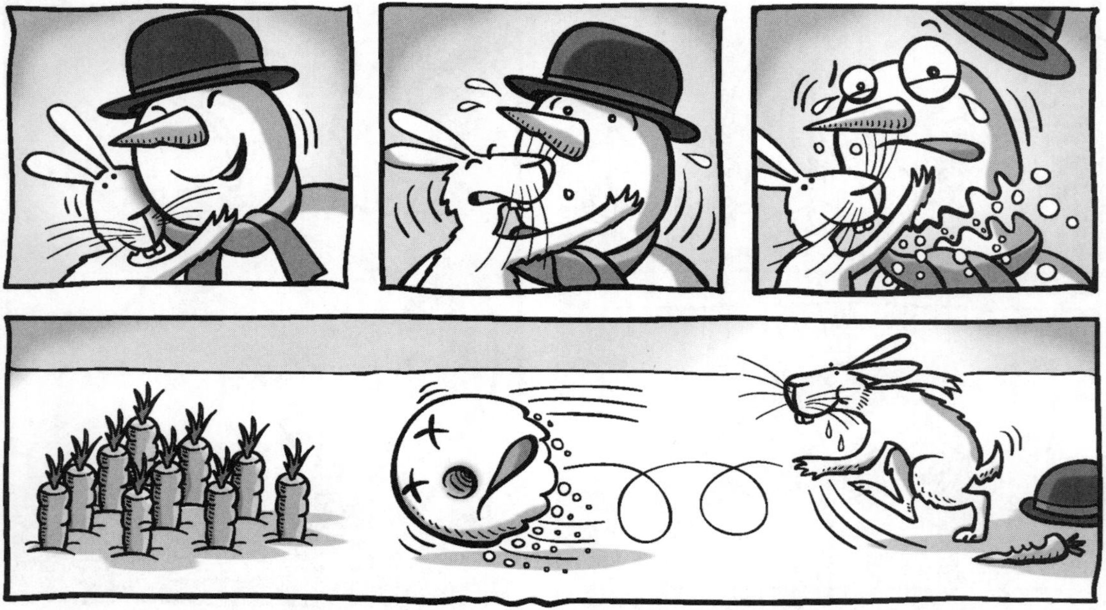

63. death by cyclist

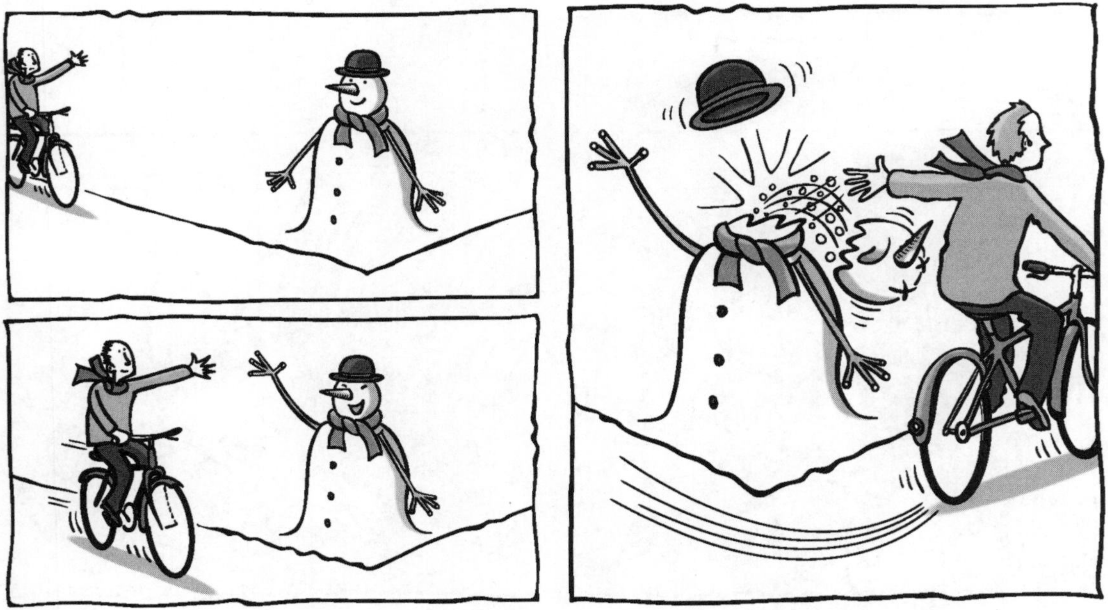

64. death by summer holiday

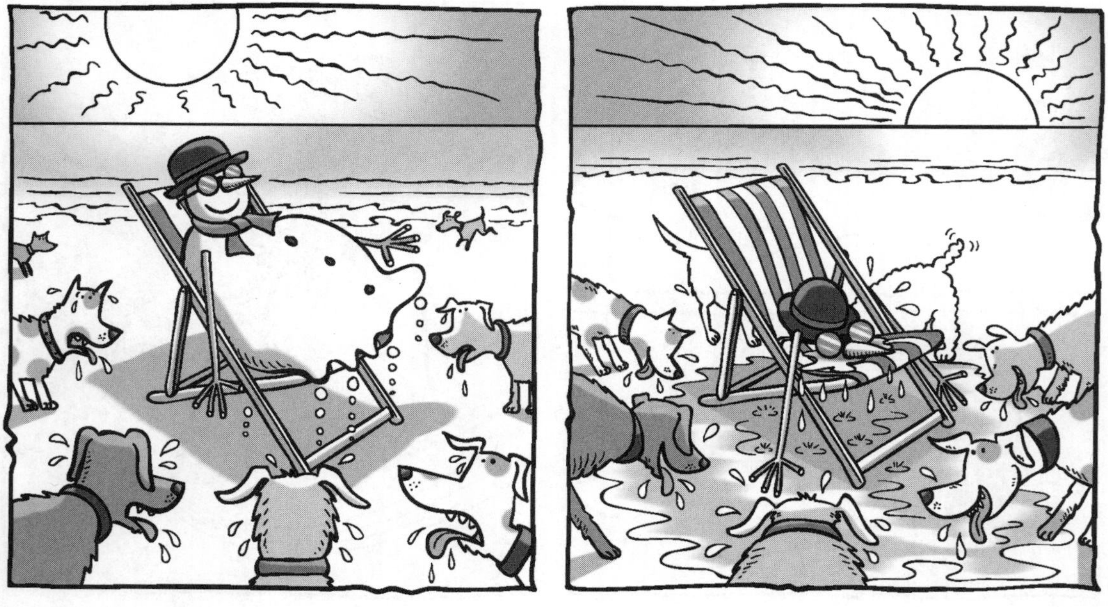

65. death by peanuts

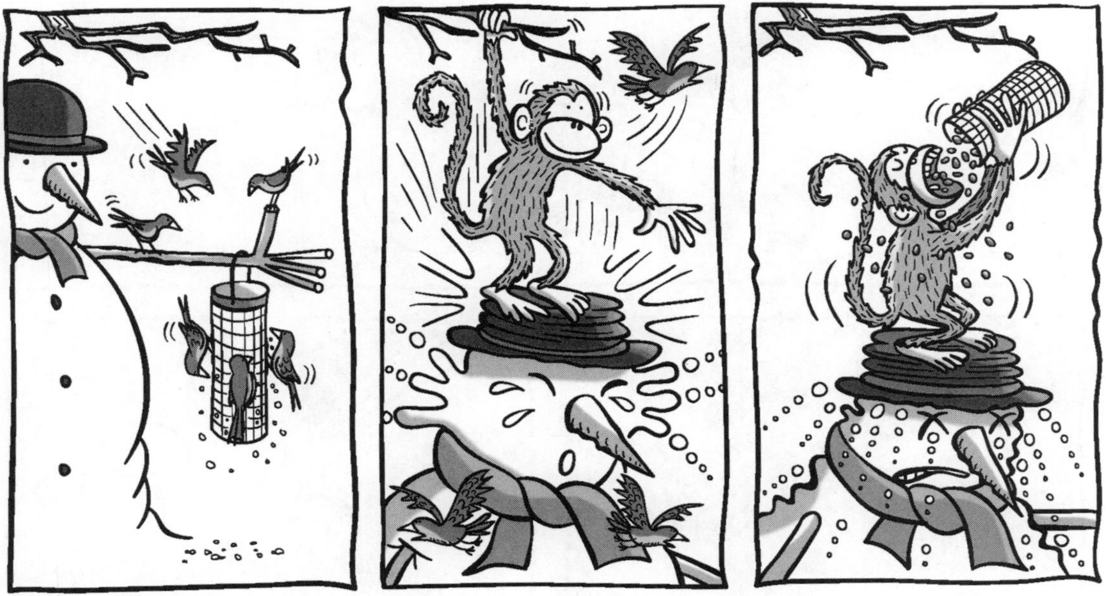

66. death by obesity no. 1

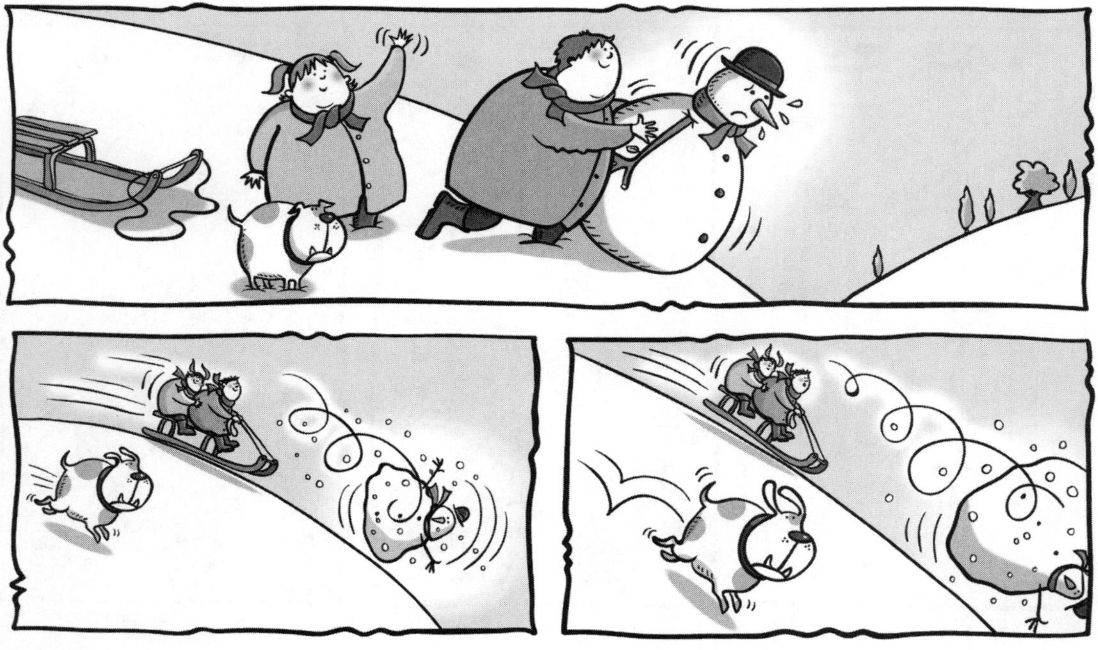

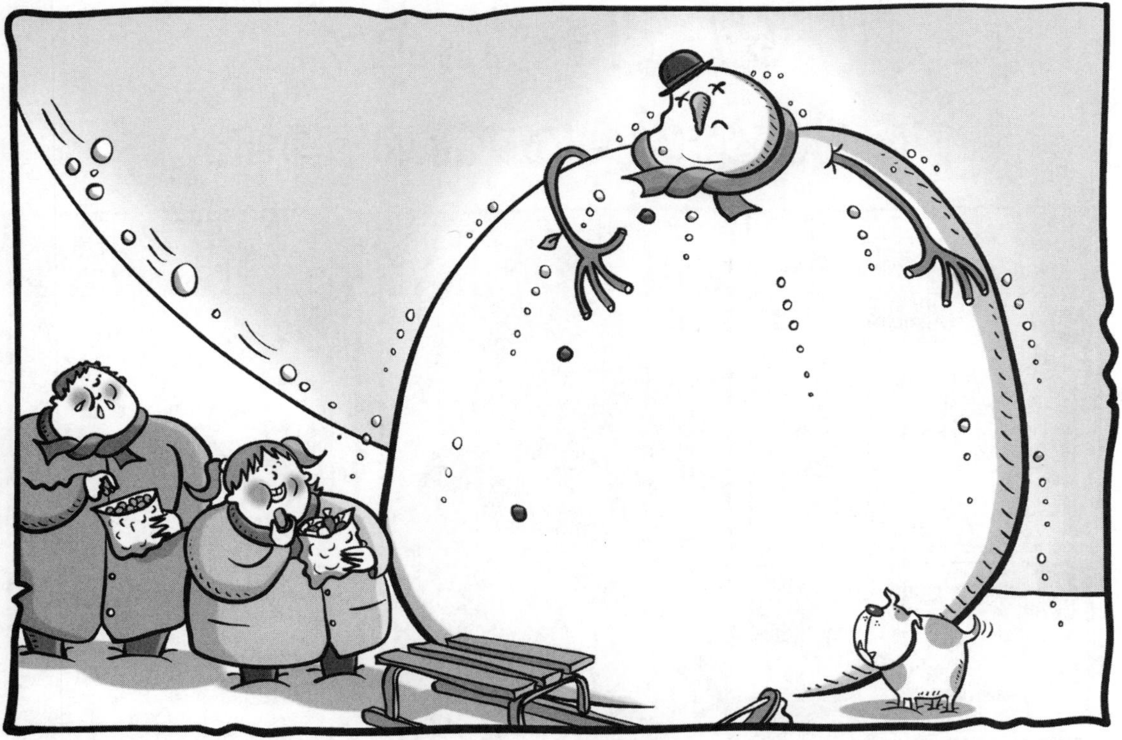

67. death by pedestrian crossing

68. death by wedding

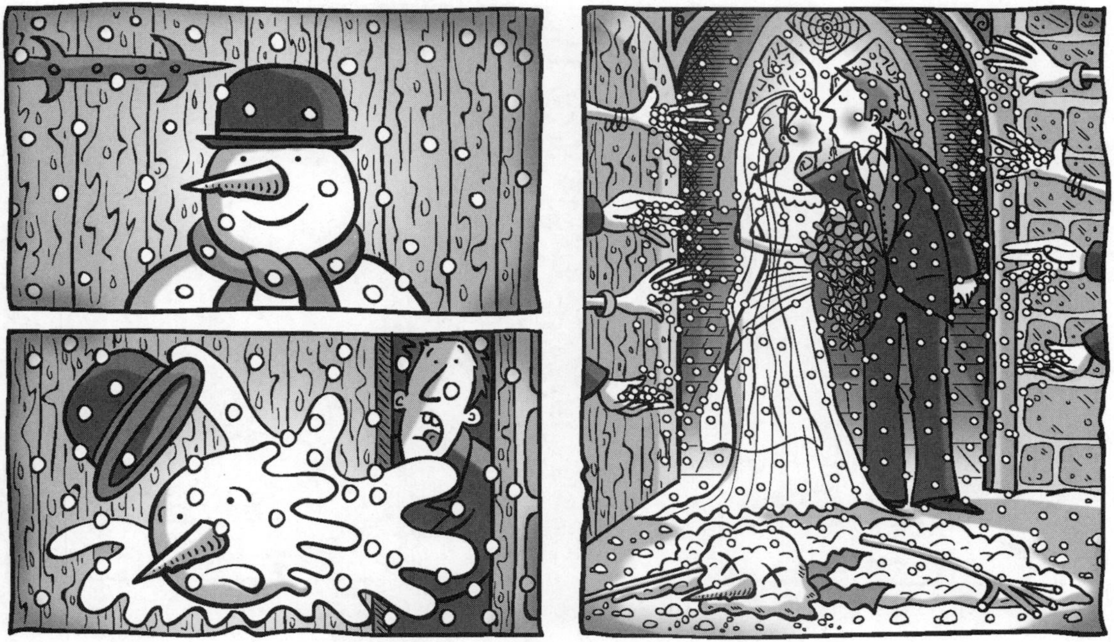

69. death by snowshaker

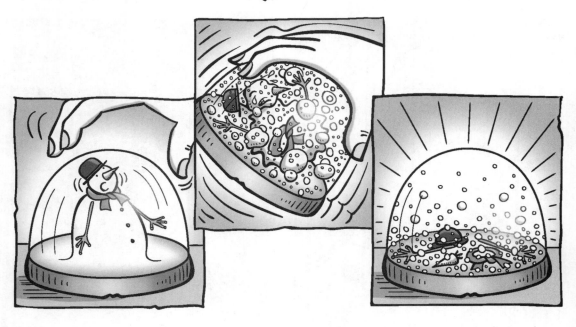

70. death by tourist

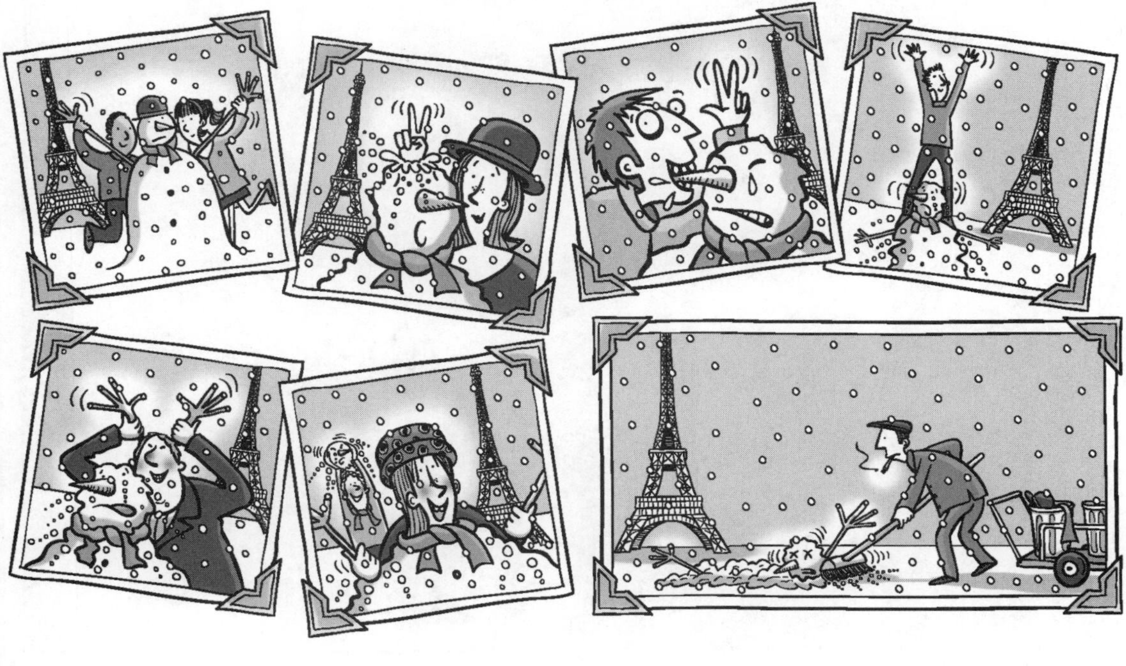

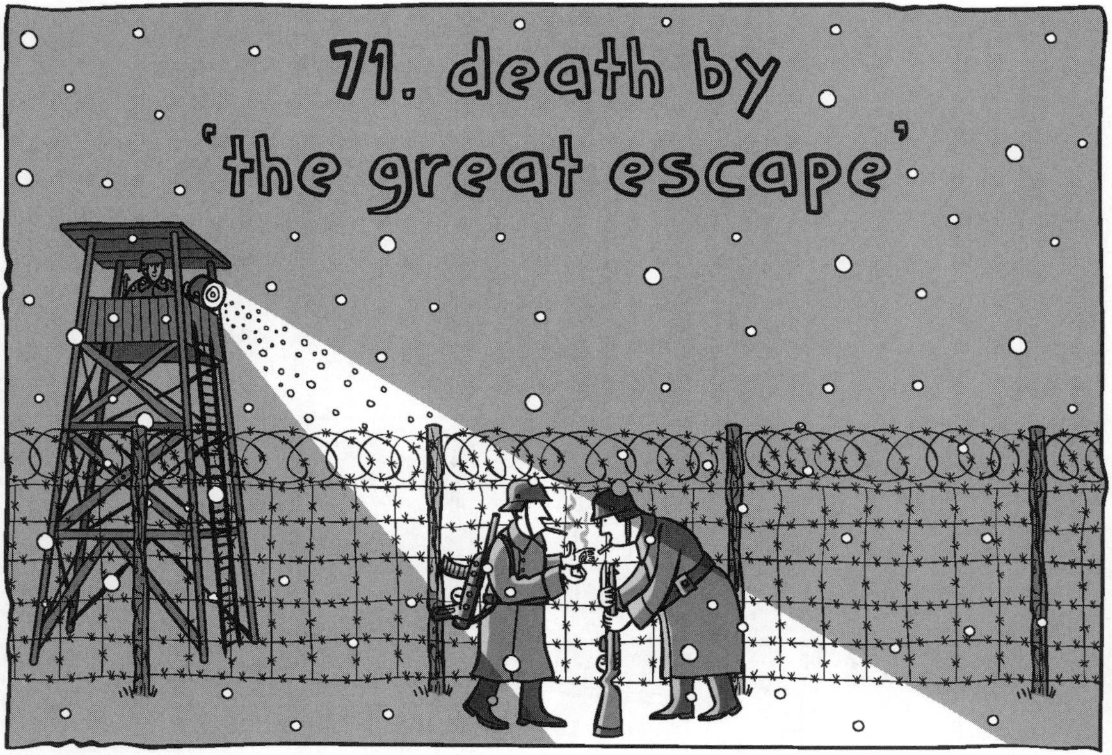
71. death by
'the great escape'

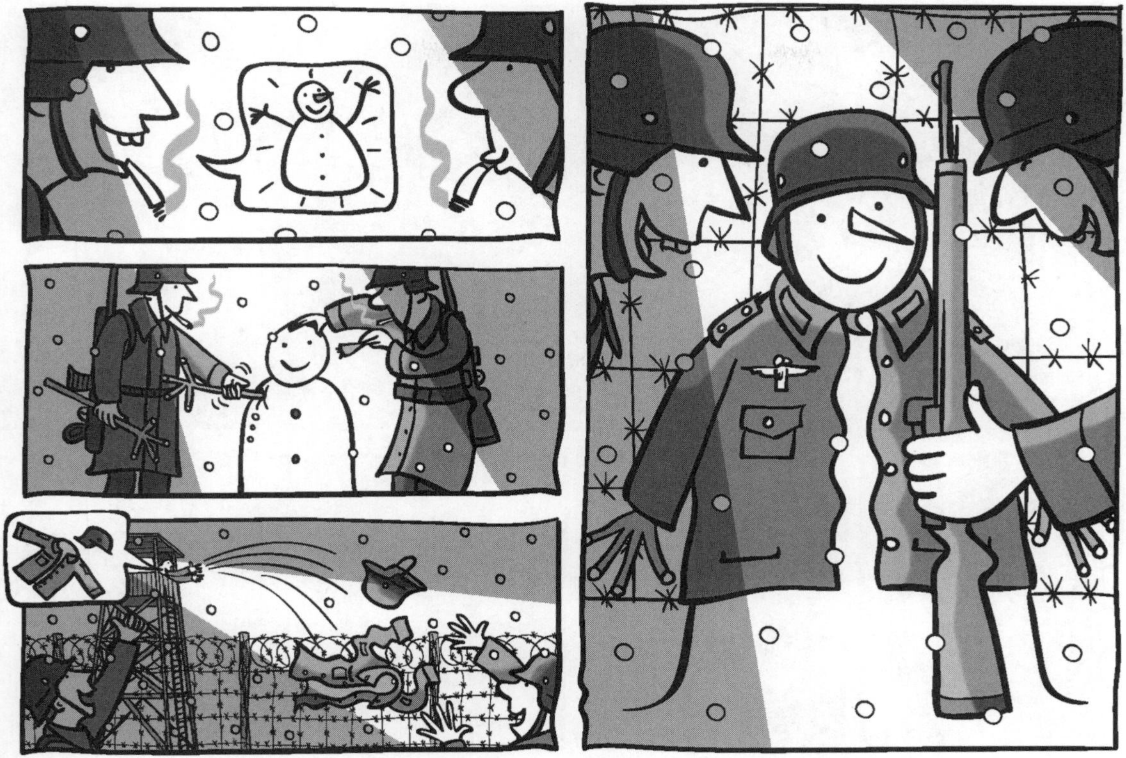

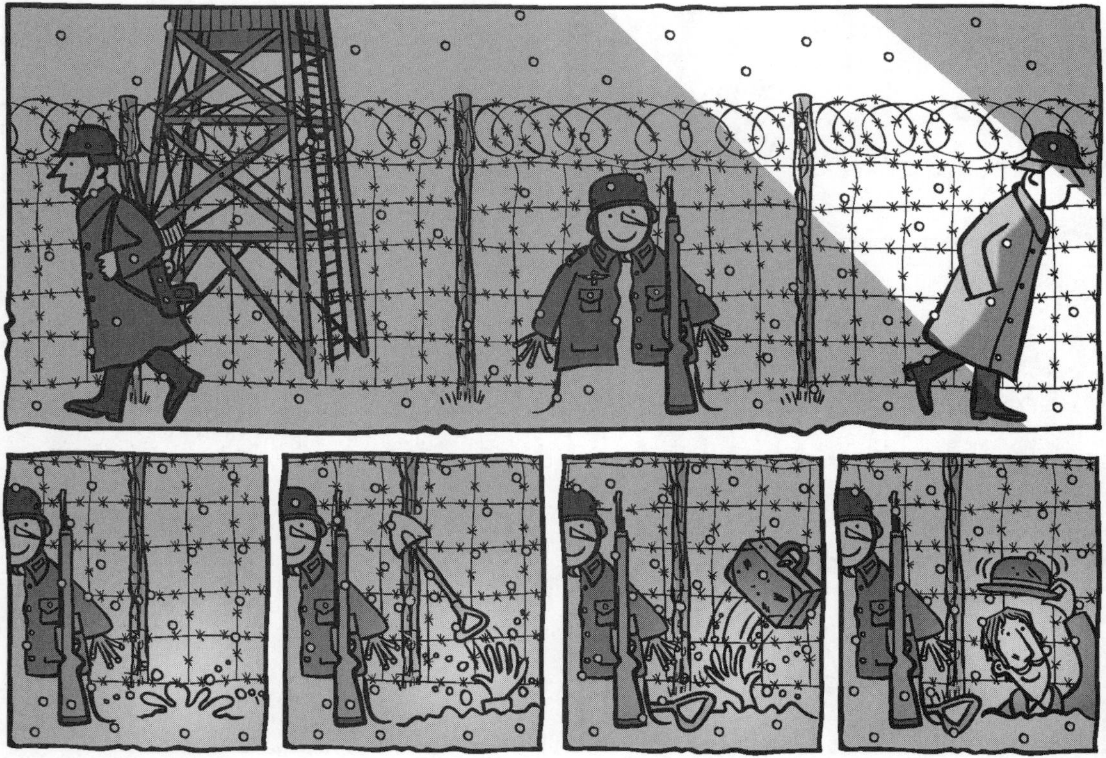

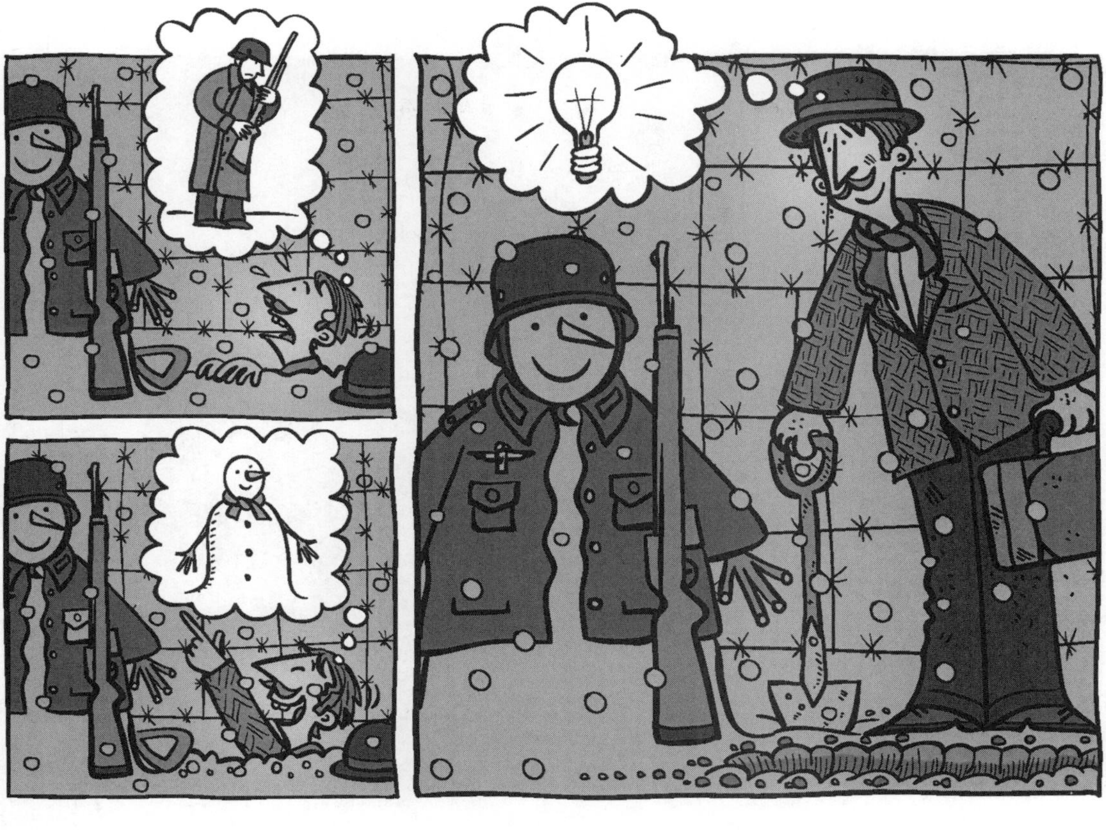

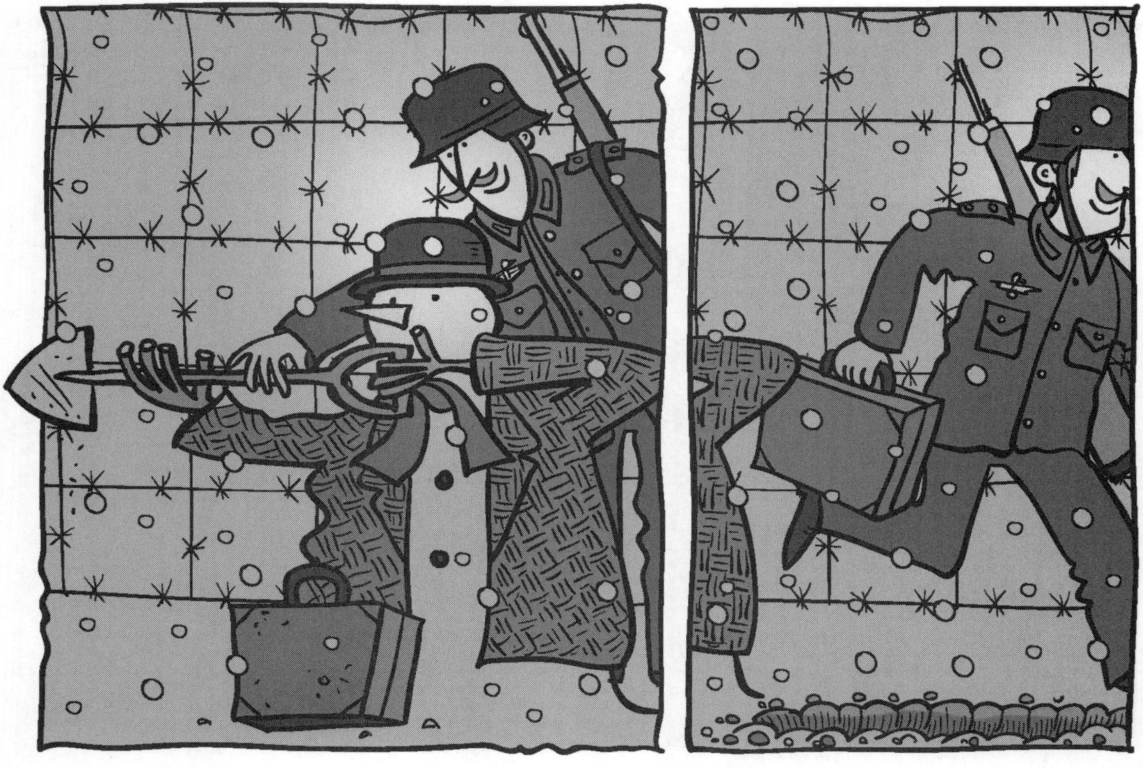

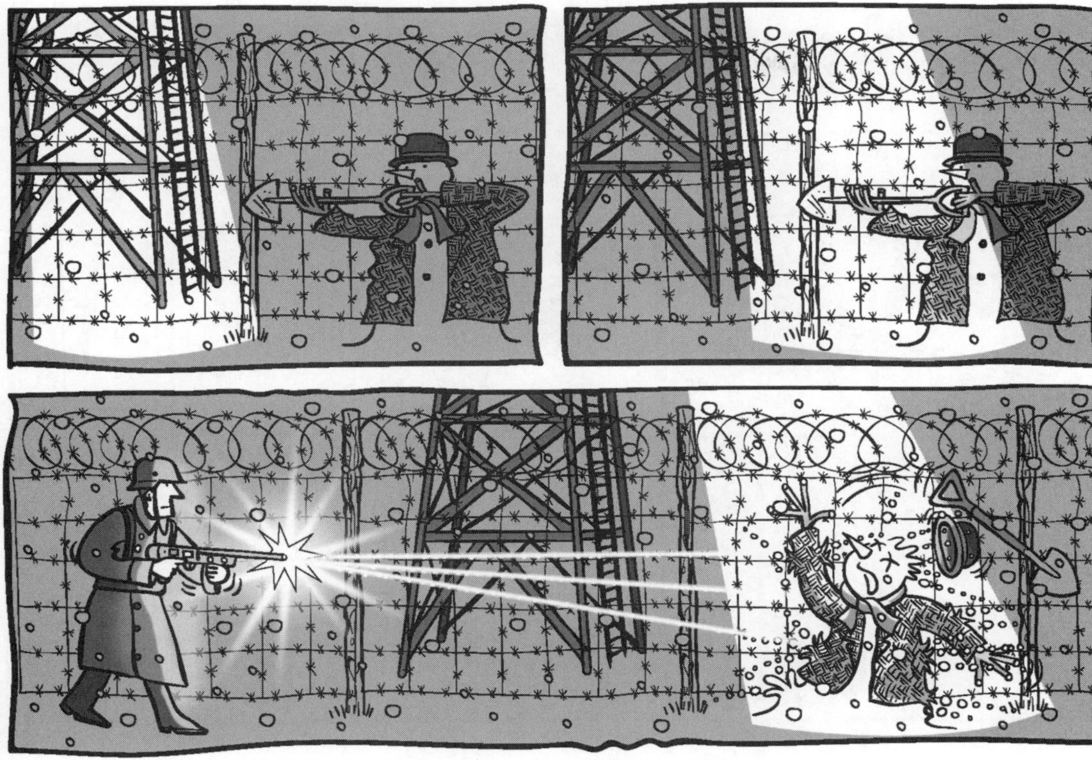

72. death by obesity no.2

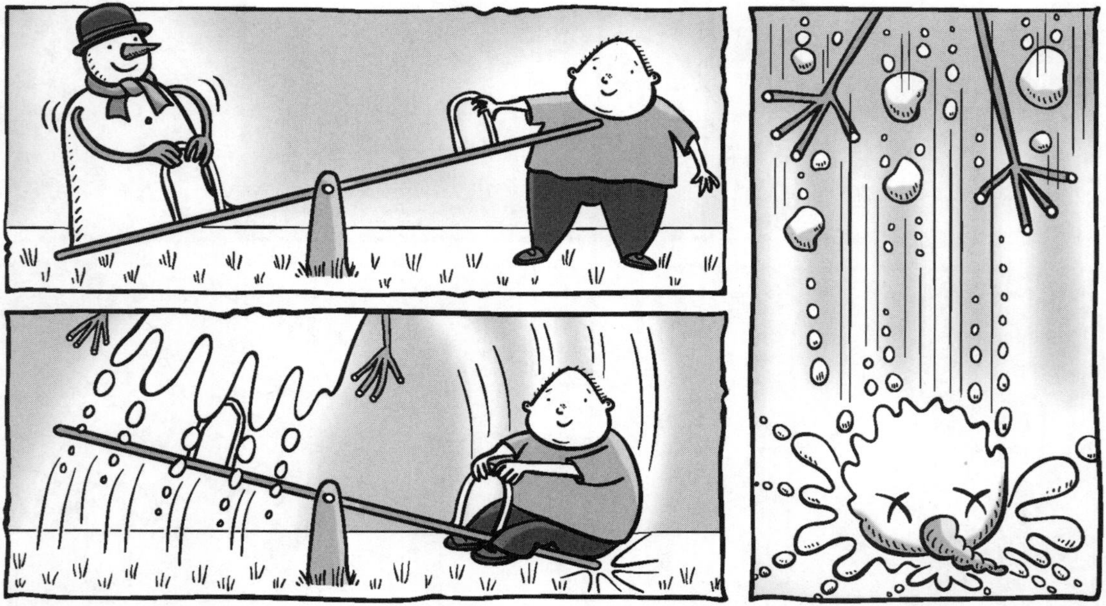

73. death by bungee jump

  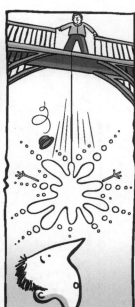 

74. death by seal

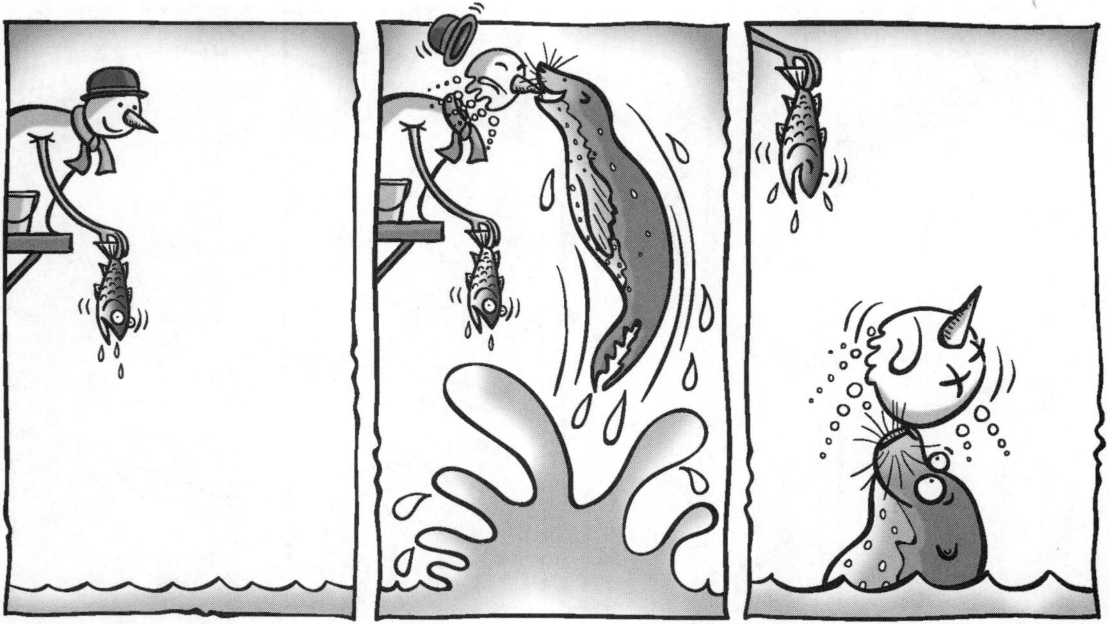

75. death by pirates

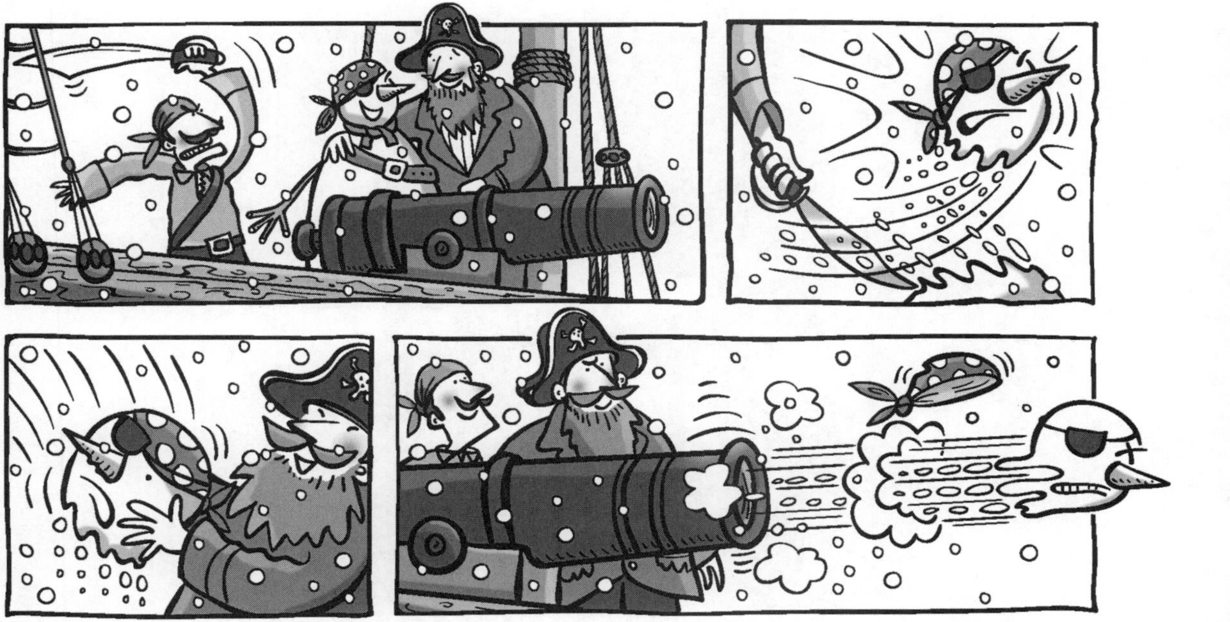

76. death by 'fire of London'

ye snowman's cottage

77. death by sea

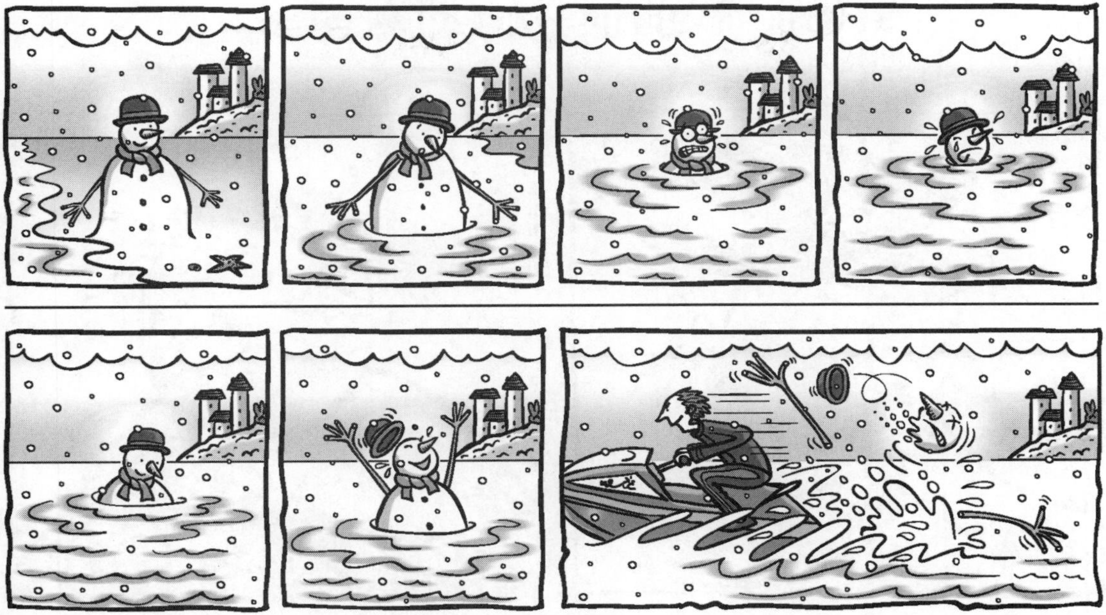

78. death by bad choice of fancy dress

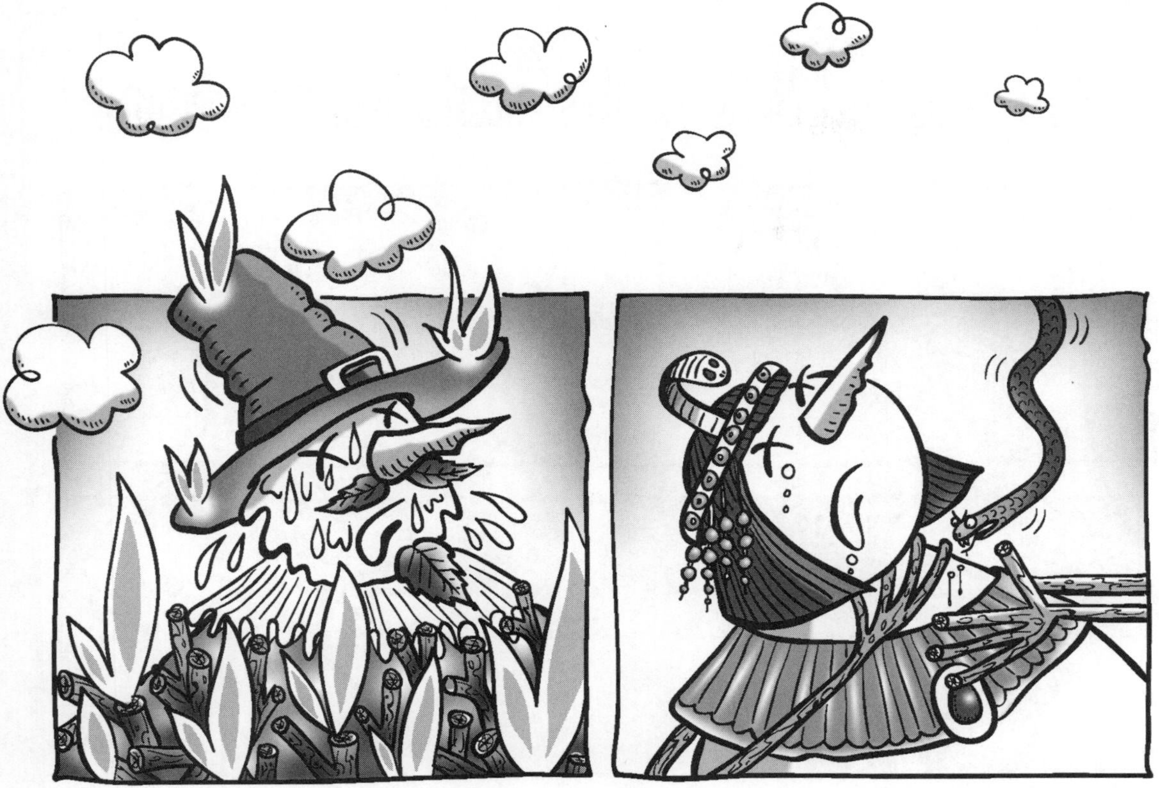

79. death by isaac newton

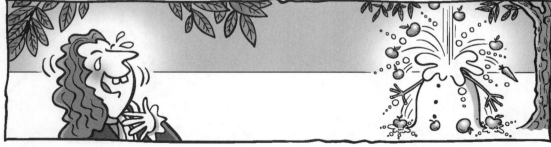

80. death by aliens (no.2)

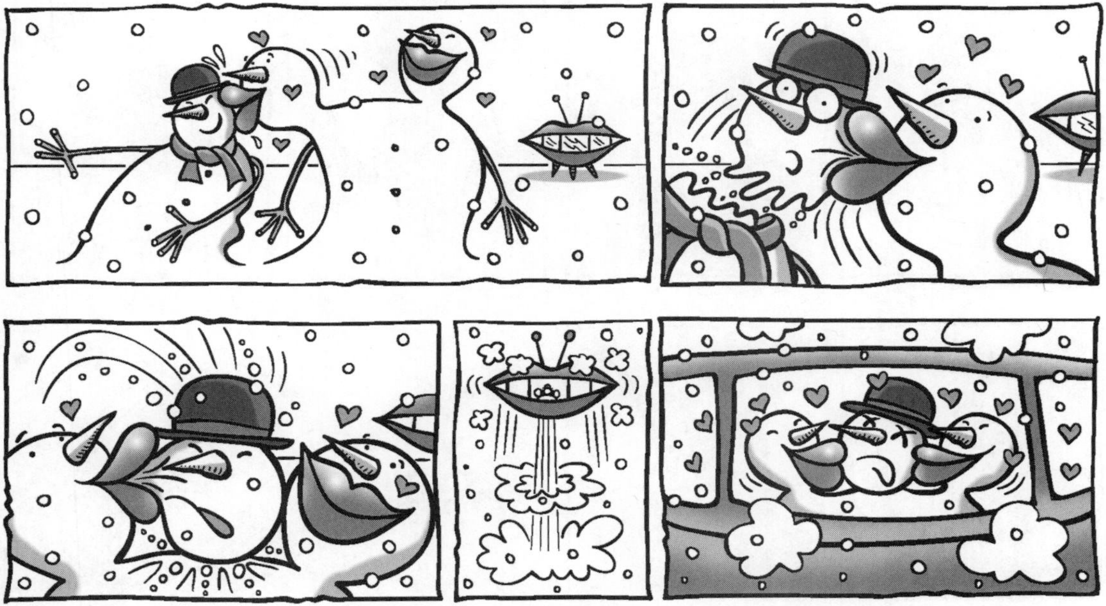

81. death by cat (no.2)

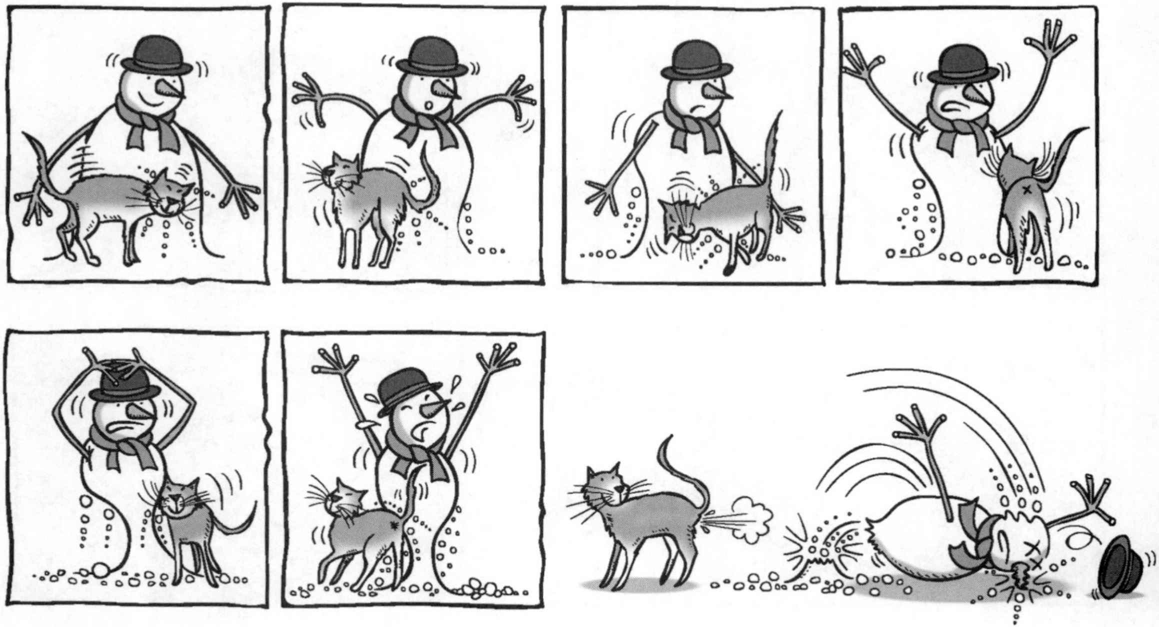

82. death by Lepidopterist

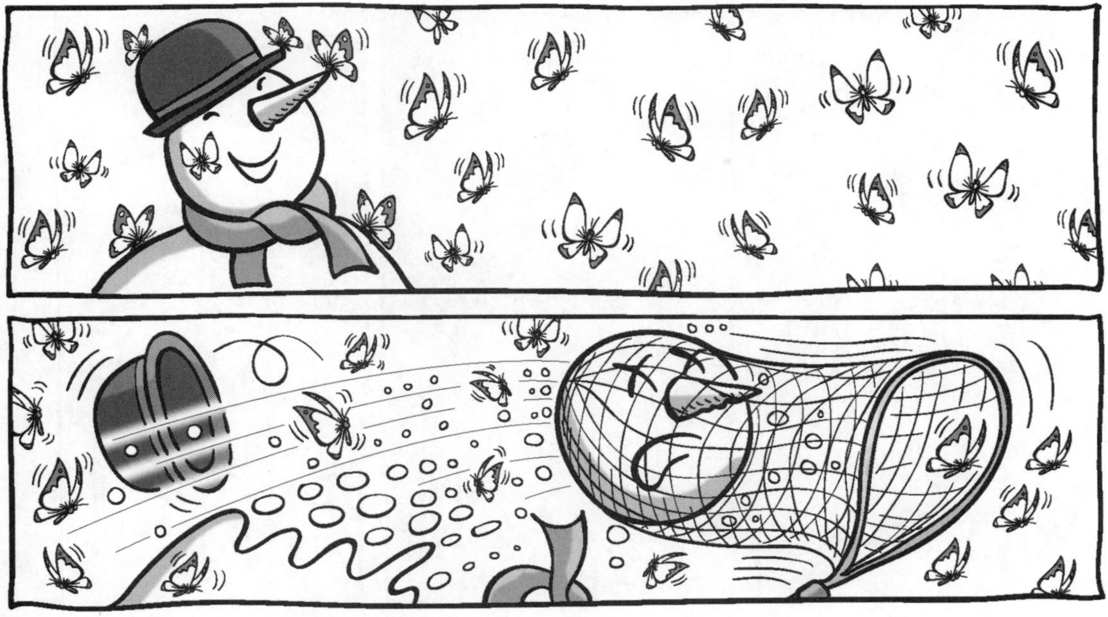

83. death by student

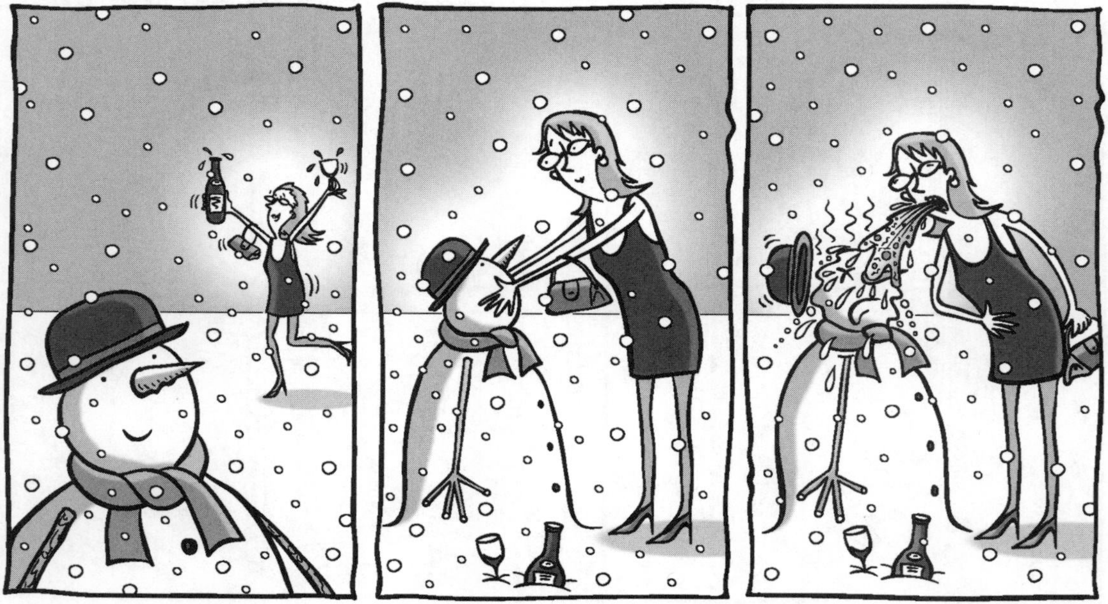

84. death by carol singers

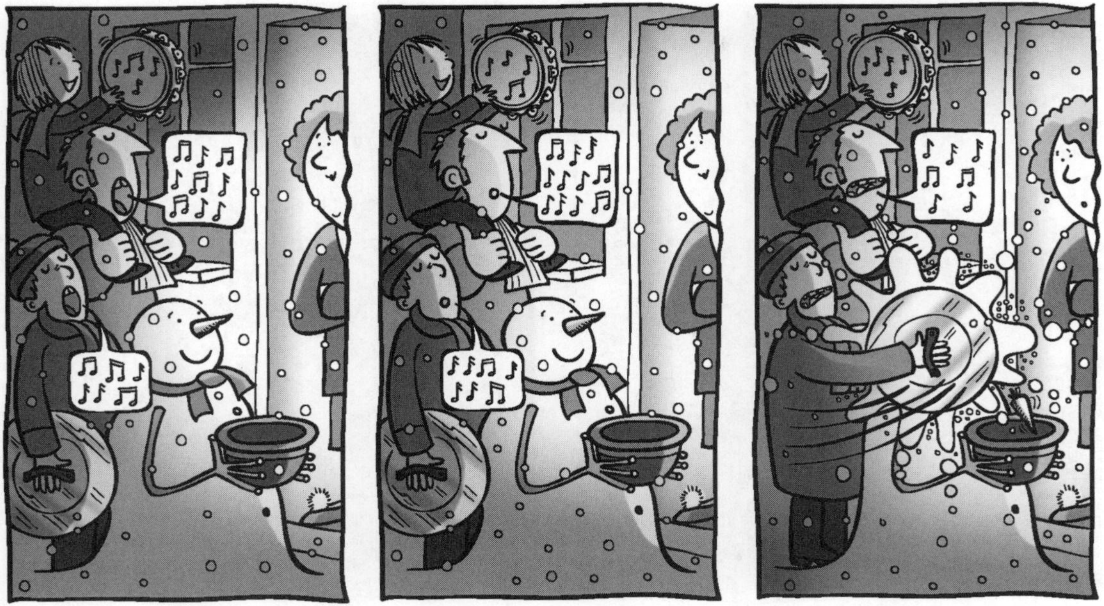

85. death by trench warfare

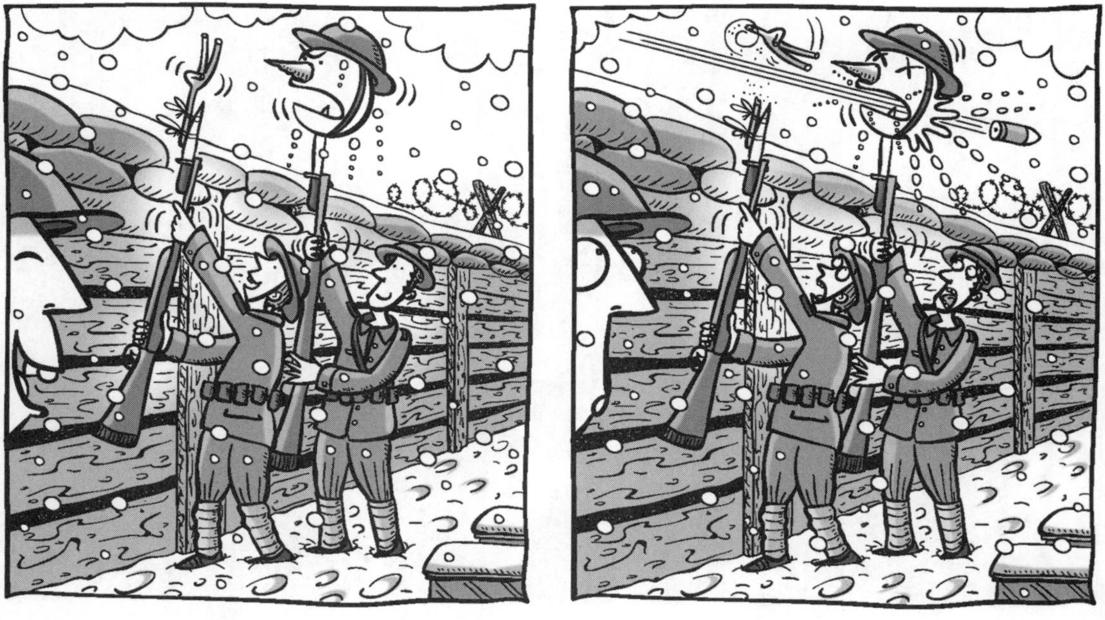

86. death by jealous caveman

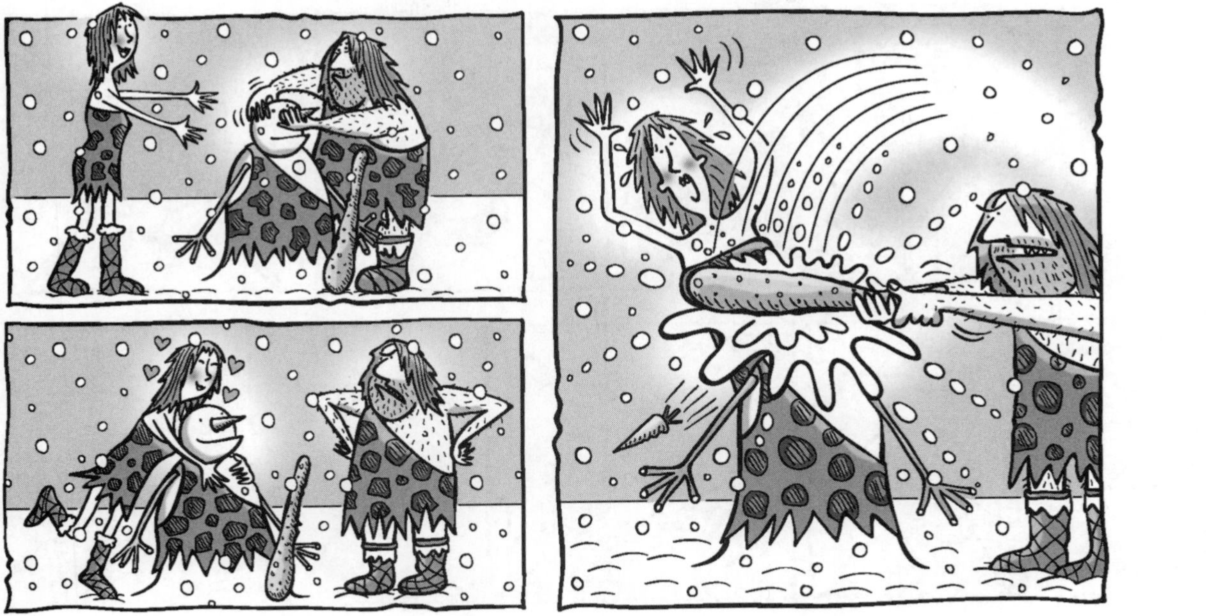

87. death by car boot sale

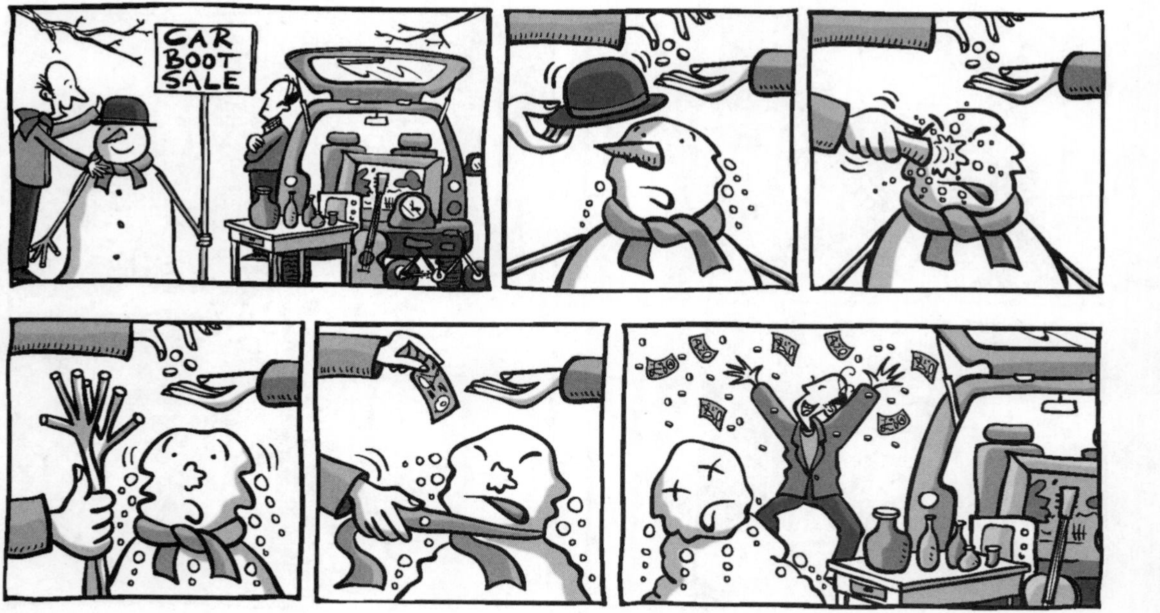
CAR
BOOT
SALE

88. death by satellite

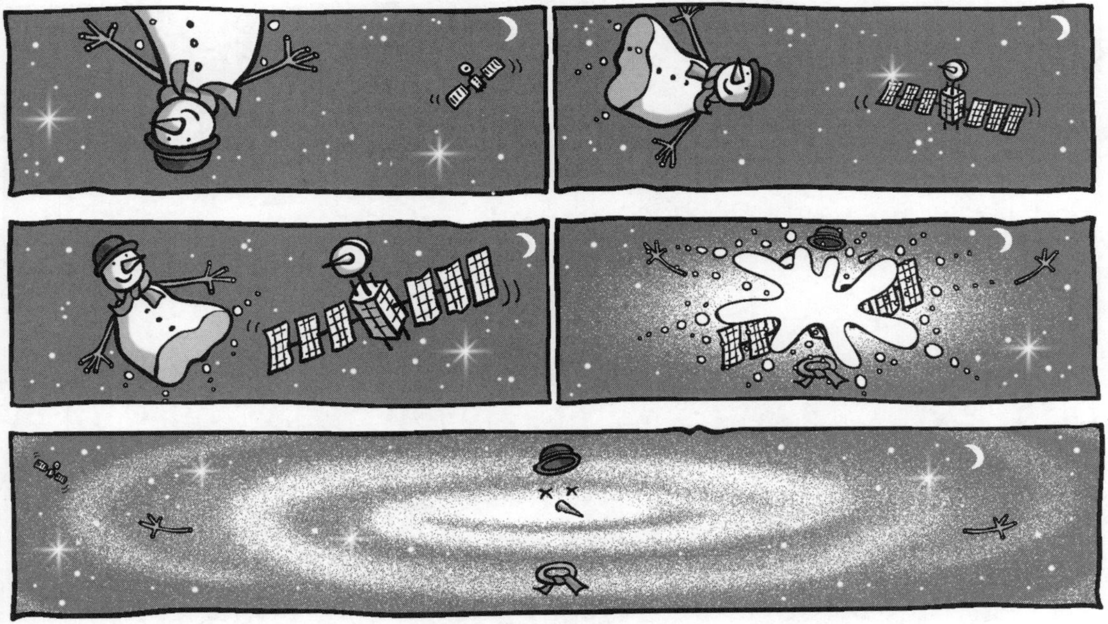

89. death by robinson crusoe

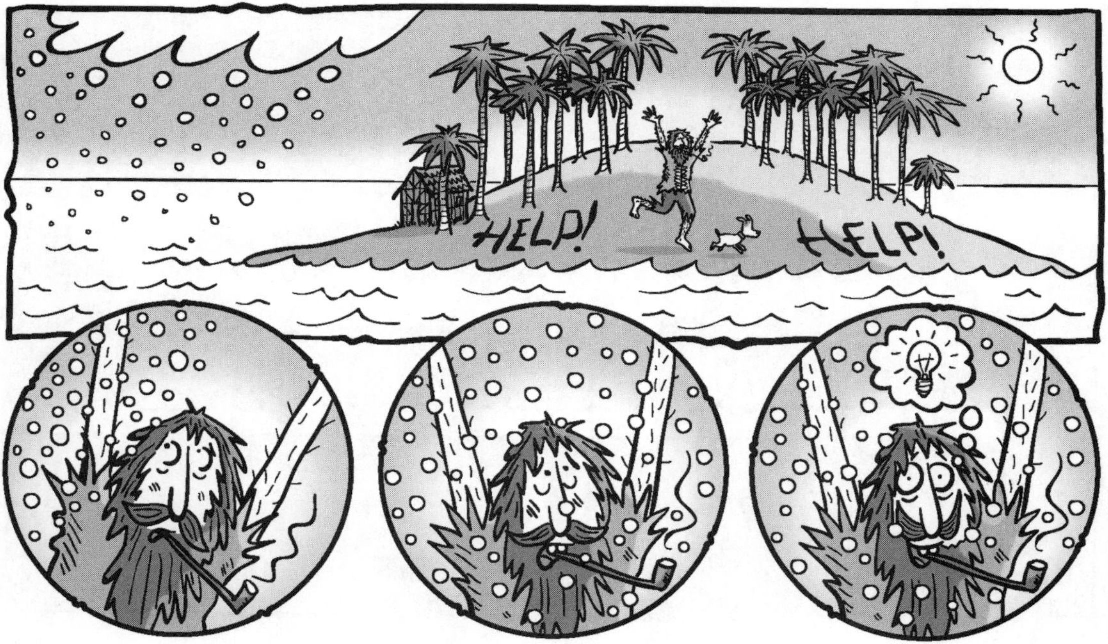
HELP!
HELP!

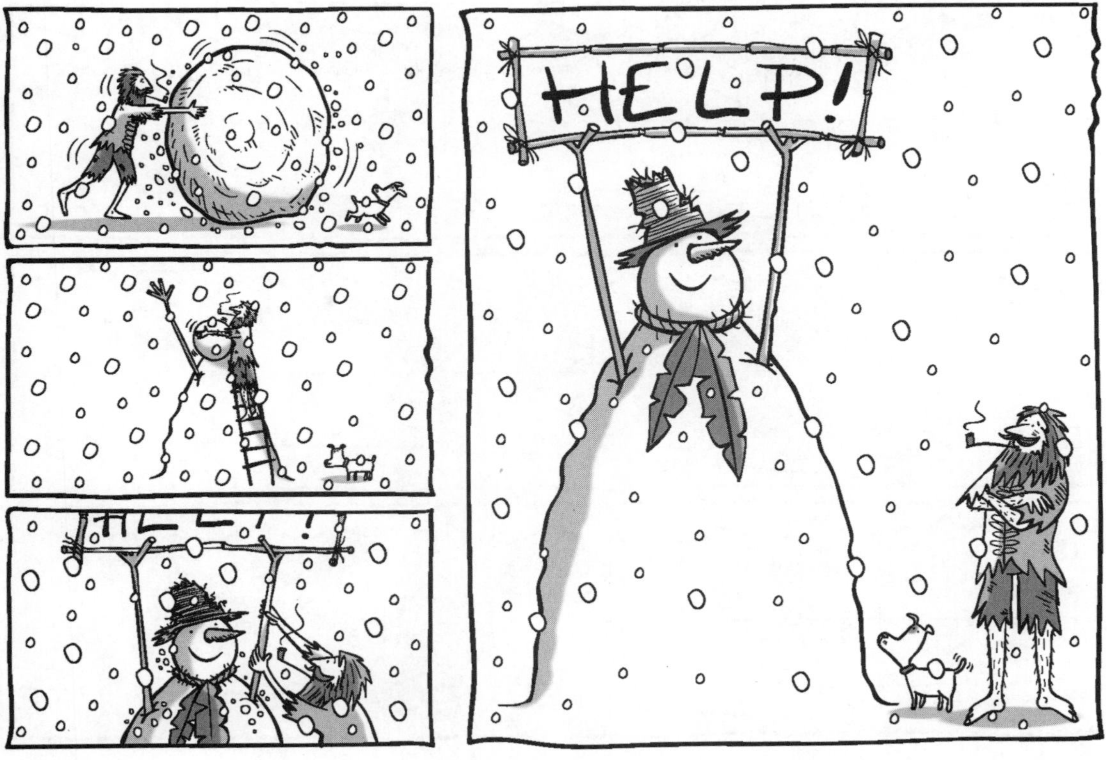
HELP!

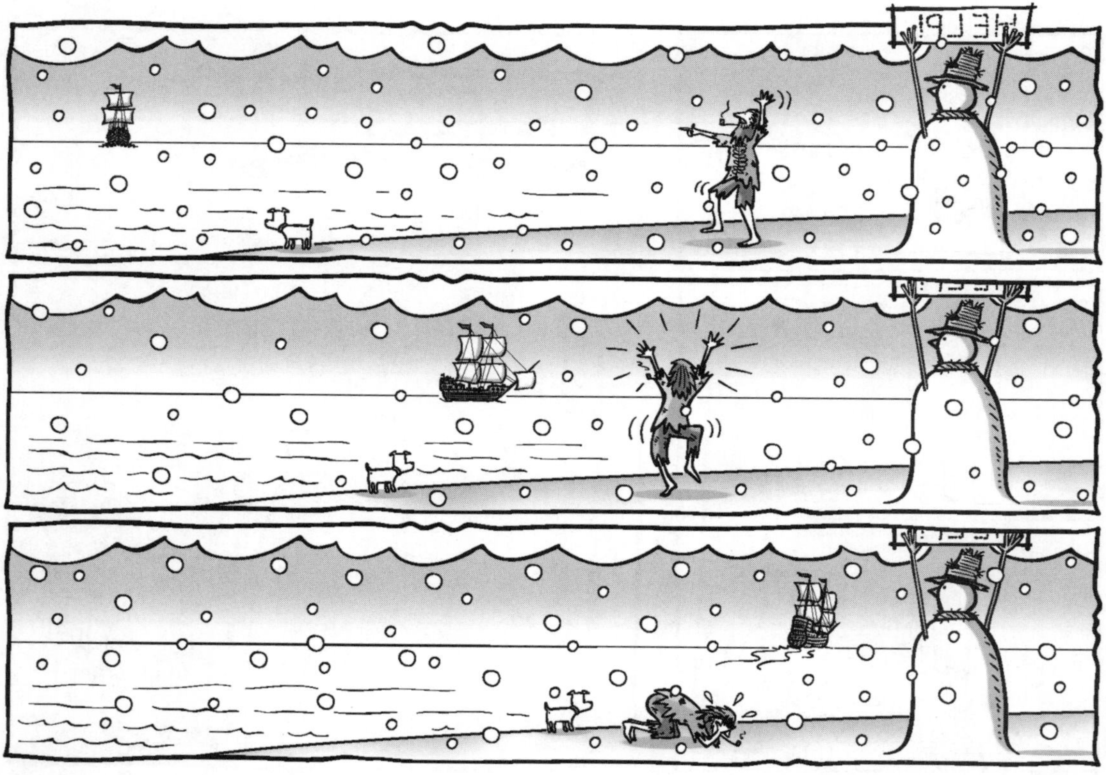
HELP!

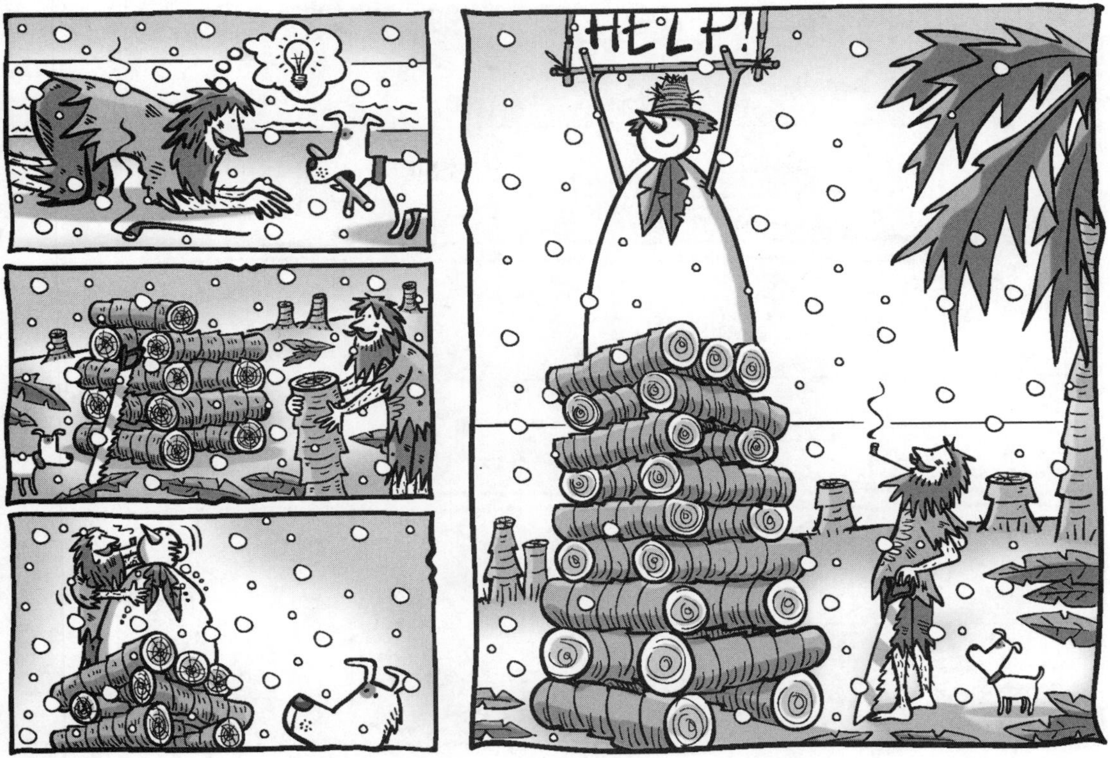
HELP!

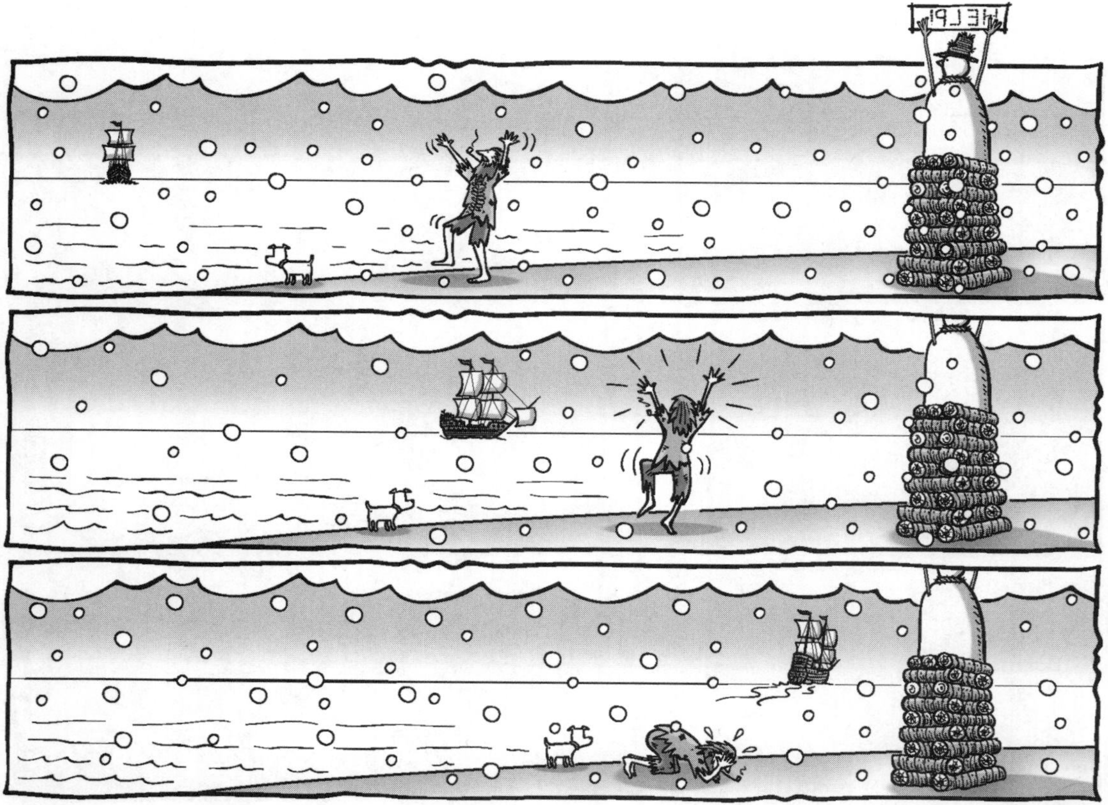
HELP!

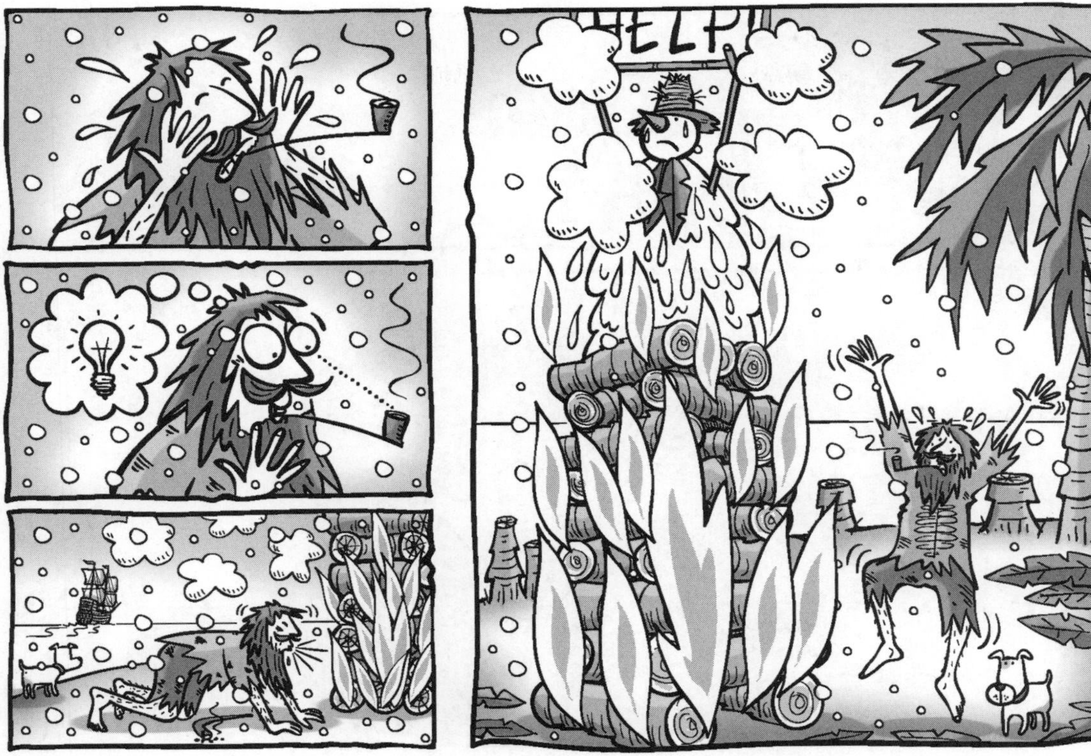

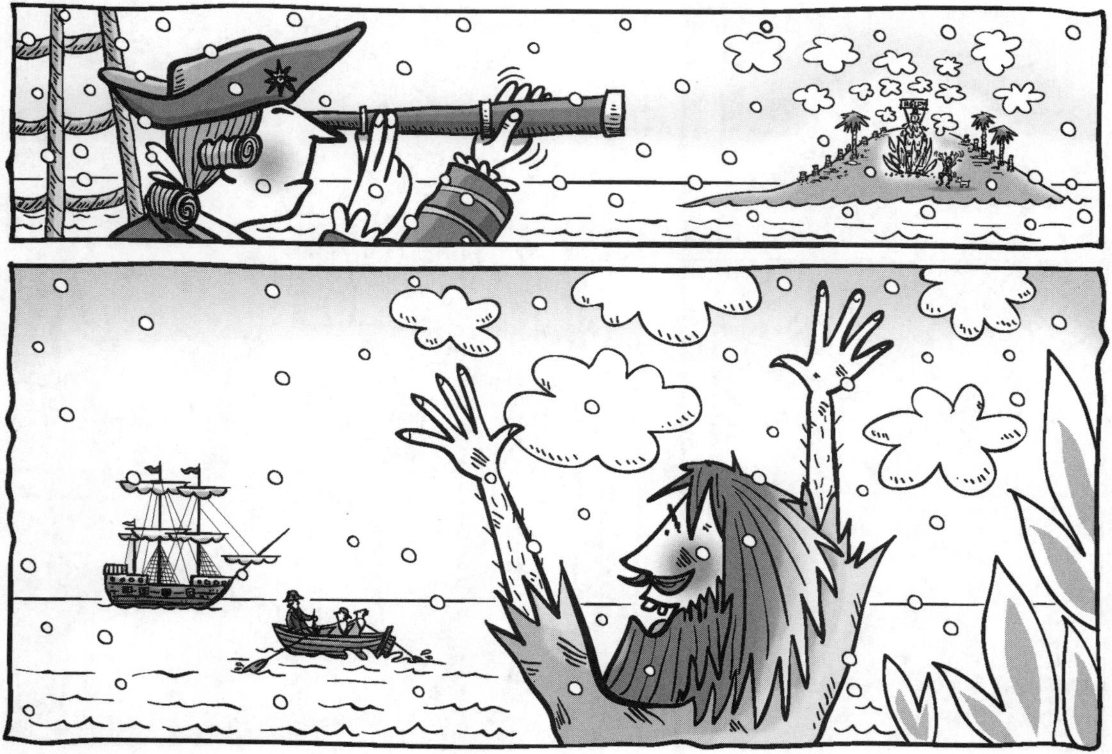

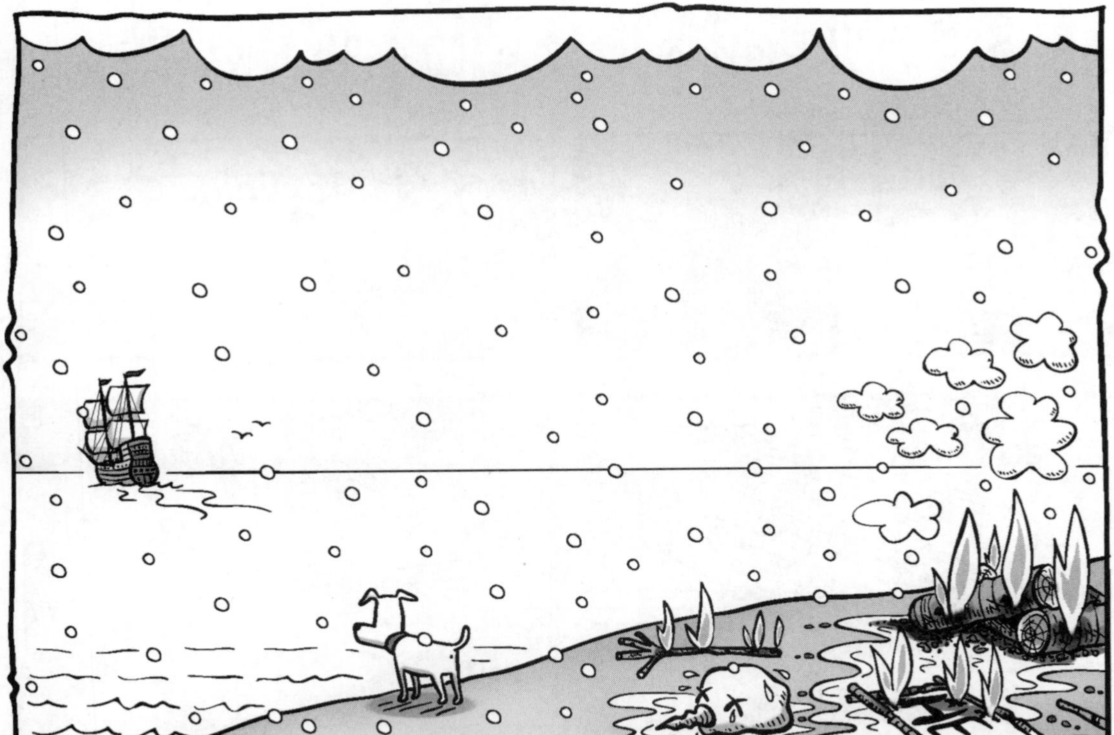

90. death by circus act

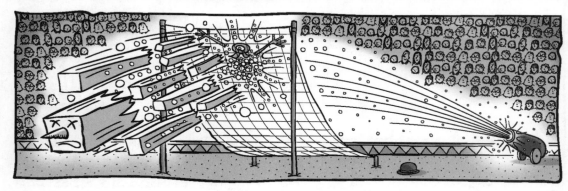

91. death by christmas pudding

92. death by busker

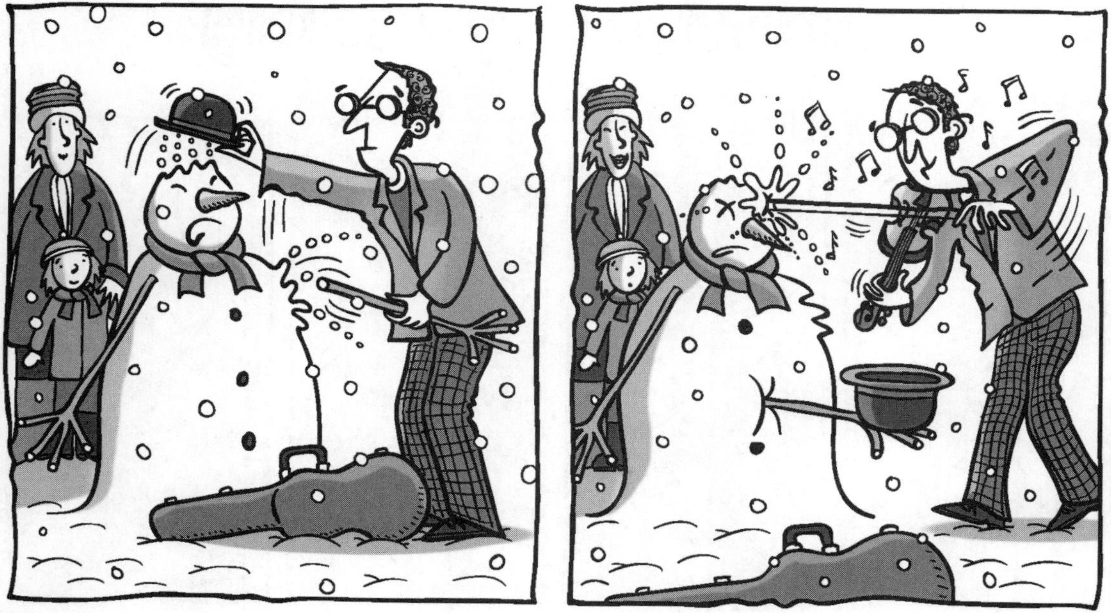

93. death by keepy uppys

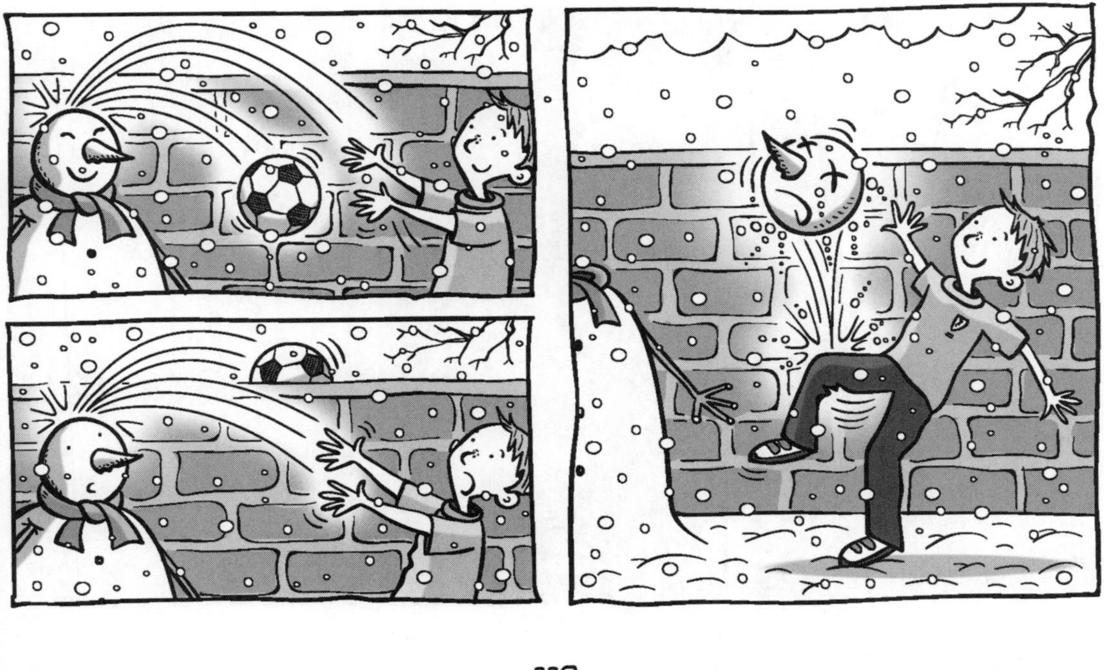

94. death by buffet

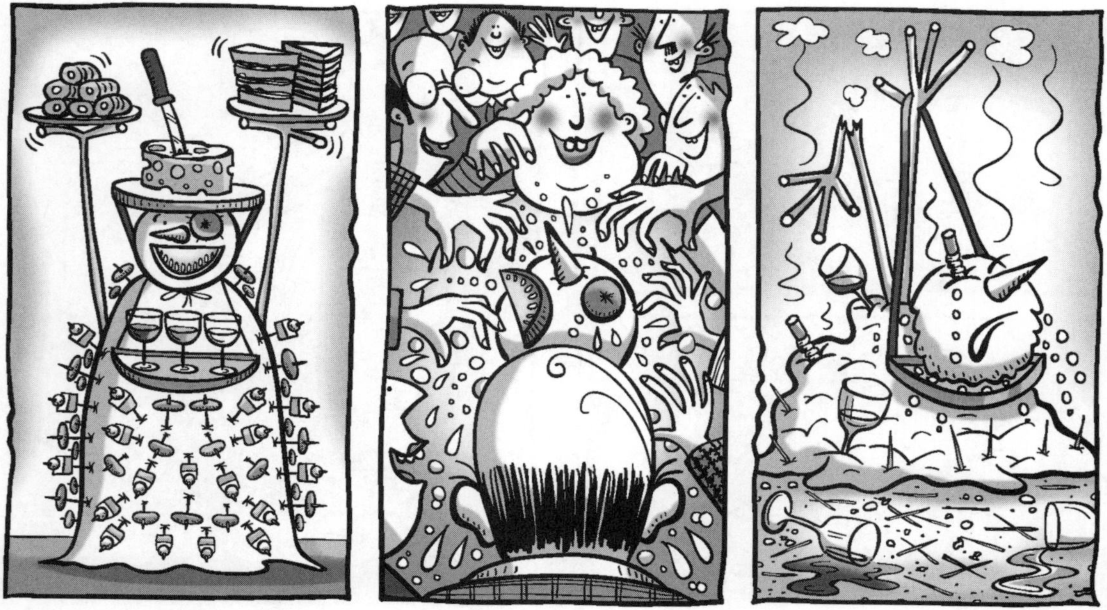

95. death by medieval excrement

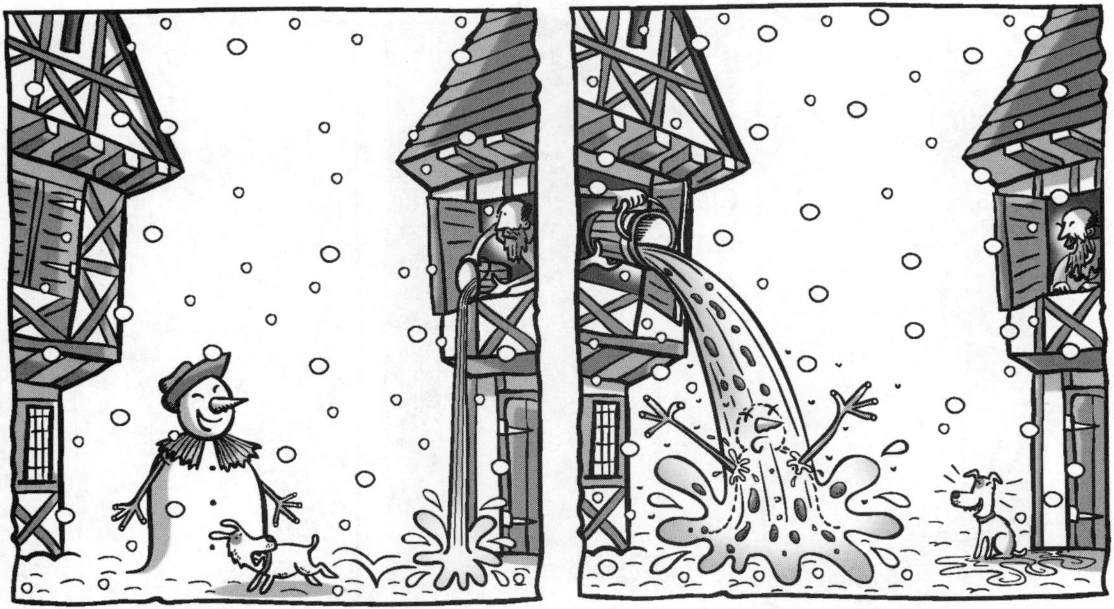

96. death by traffic warden

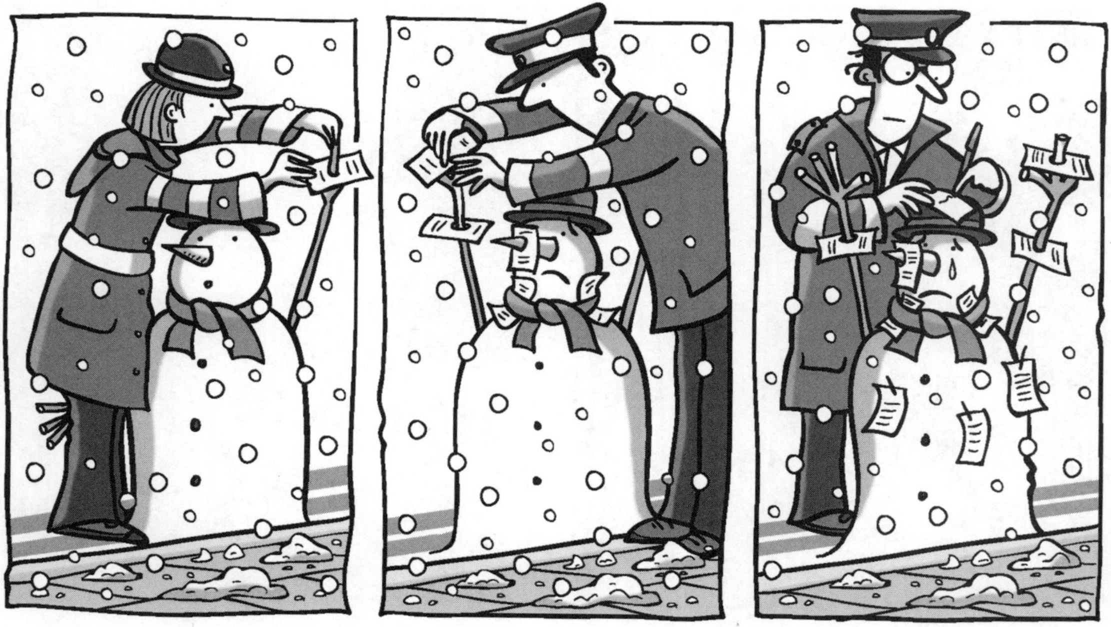

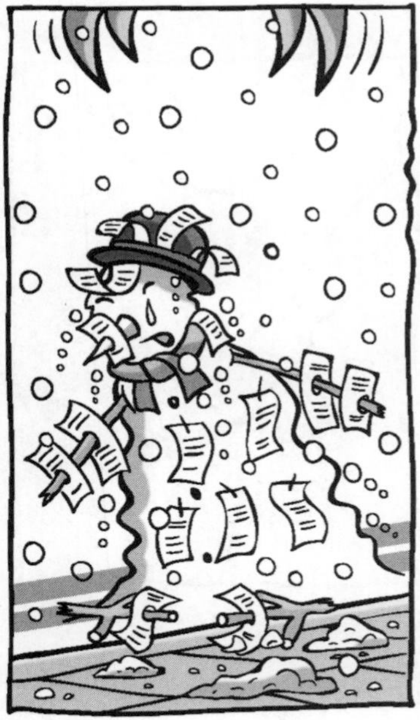

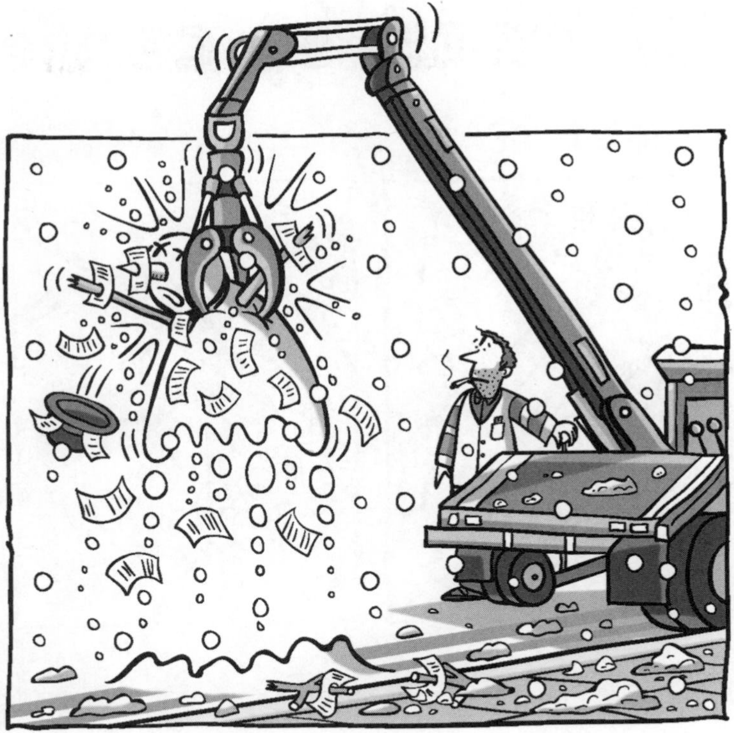

97. death by confectionary

98. death by sub

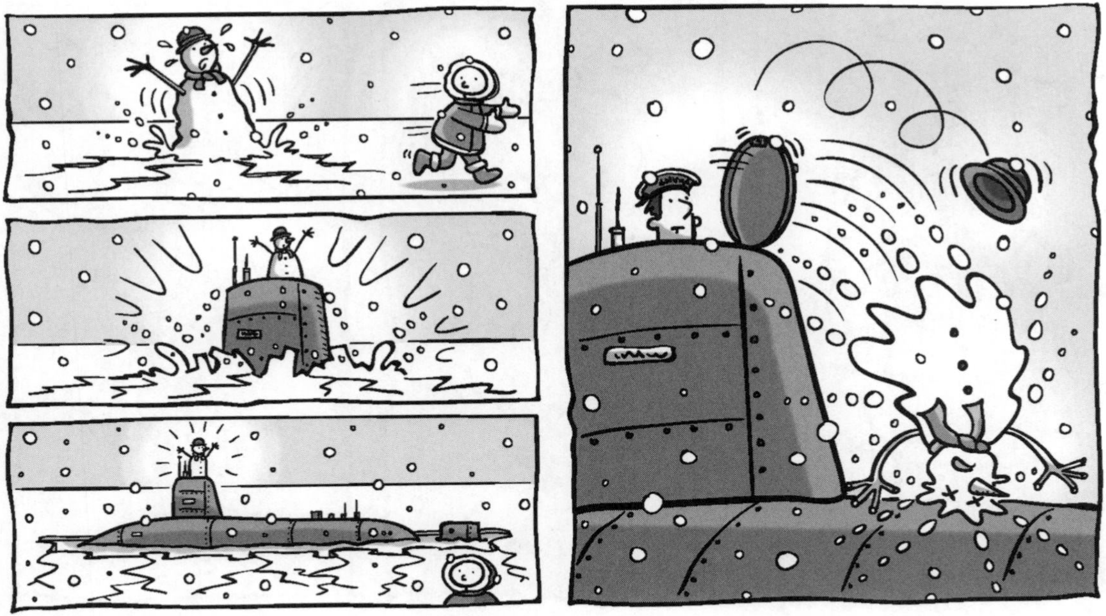

99. death by rabbit (no.4)

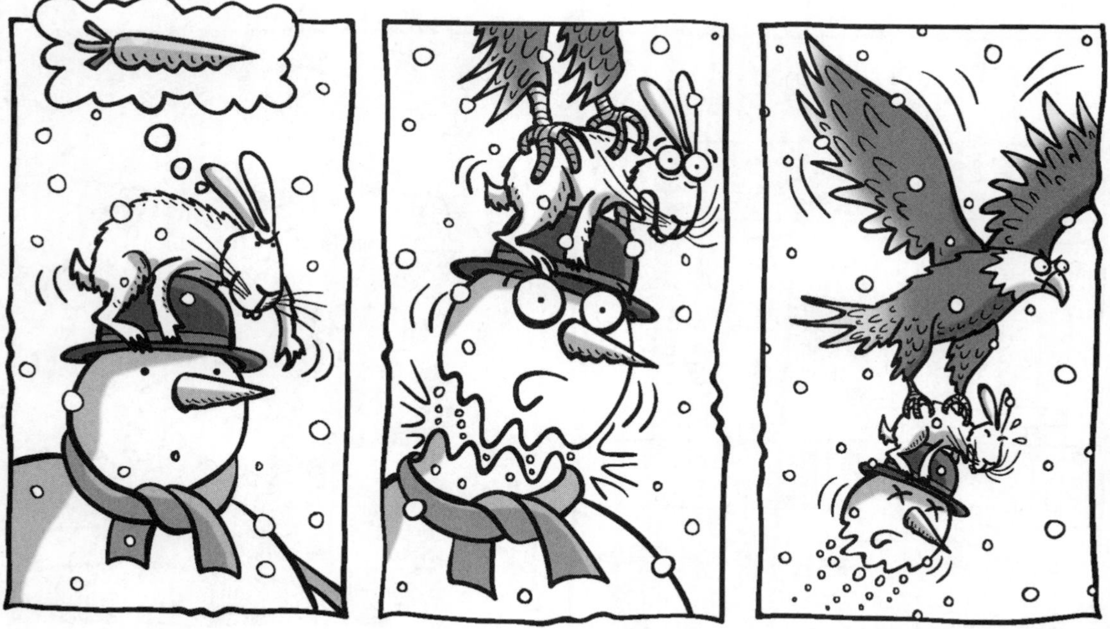

100. back from the dead...

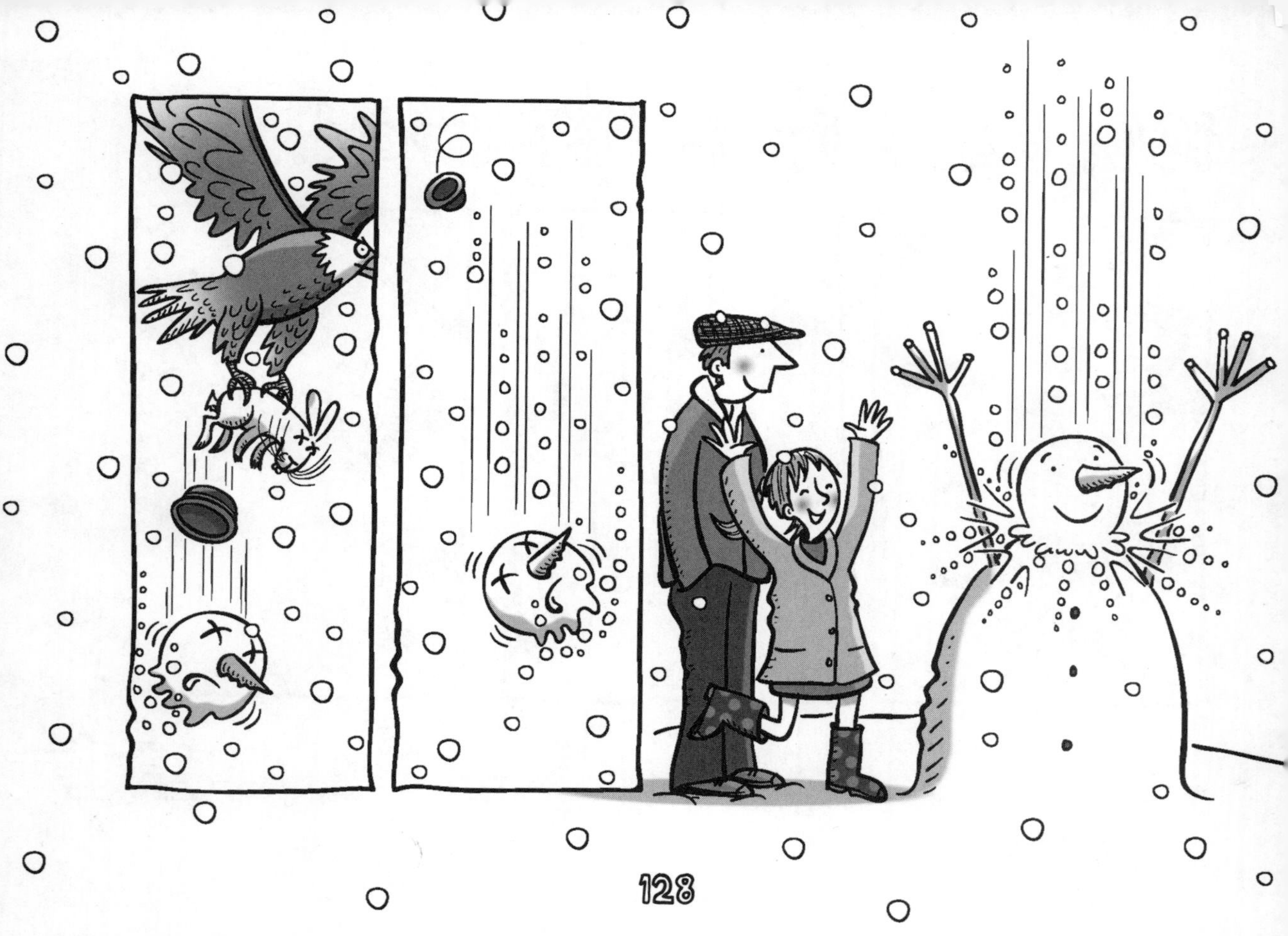